A KITCHEN IN FRANCE

A KITCHEN IN FRANCE

A Year of Cooking in My Farmhouse

MIMI THORISSON

Photographs by Oddur Thorisson

CLARKSON POTTER/PUBLISHERS

New York

Published in the United States by Clarkson Potter/Publishers, an imprint
of the Crown Publishing Group, a division of Random House LLC, a Penguin
Random House Company, New York.
www.crownpublishing.com
www.clarksonpotter.com

CLARKSON POTTER is a trademark and POTTER with colophon is a registered
trademark of Random House LLC.

Library of Congress Cataloging-in-Publication Data
Thorisson, Mimi.
A Kitchen in France : a year of cooking in my farmhouse / Mimi Thorisson ;
photographs by Oddur Thorisson.
    pages cm
  Includes index.
  1. Cooking, French. 2. Cooking—France—Médoc. 3. Seasonal cooking—
France—Médoc. 4. Thorisson, Mimi—Homes and haunts—France—Médoc.
5. Farmhouses—France—Médoc. 6. Seasons—France—Médoc. 7. Médoc
(France)—Social life and customs. 8. Médoc (France)—Biography. 9. Médoc
(France) —Description and travel. I. Title.

TX719.T473 2014   641.5944'714—dc23   2013049107

ISBN 978-0-8041-8559-2
eBook ISBN 978-0-8041-8560-8

Printed in China

Book and jacket design by
JENNIFER K. BEAL DAVIS

Jacket photography by
ODDUR THORISSON

Illustrations by
ANNA RIFLE BOND

10 9 8 7 6 5 4 3 2 1

First Edition

FOR MY FAMILY

CONTENTS

INTRODUCTION

If you are not capable of a bit of witchcraft,
don't trouble yourself with cooking.
—Colette

There is a ferry that sails south from the town of Royan, on the Atlantic Ocean, to Le Verdon at the northern tip of the Médoc peninsula. It is not a particularly charming ride—nor one I had ever planned on taking. Yet one day in late autumn some years ago, I found myself on that ferry with my husband, three kids, five dogs, and a baby on the way. We had given up our apartment in the lovely 7th arrondissement of Paris, found a house in Médoc, and, voilà, there we were.

How did an only child from bustling Hong Kong, born into a family with a fondness for cats, whose French mother hardly ever set foot in the kitchen, end up on that ferry? I don't know exactly, but I think my current country lifestyle—complete with a big rowdy family, lots of dogs, and a huge kitchen where I can make

all my culinary fantasies come true—is something I always wanted.

My favorite food memories of my childhood include my father taking me, sometimes late at night, to little food stalls in Hong Kong. We'd seek out the best tripe, the finest dumplings, our favorite comforting bowl of noodles. I was a picky eater, a skinny child, which drove him nuts. But in the end he always found a way to feed my cravings. He probably understood me better than anyone; I definitely inherited my food obsession from him. We didn't say hello, but, instead, "Have you eaten?" as many Chinese people do.

In contrast, we spent our holidays in Paris or in the south of France with my mother's family. There I was introduced to a whole other world of tastes and flavors, a new universe of gastronomic delights. My grandmother and aunt were both terrific cooks, and every day meant a feast. We started many mornings with a trip to Monsieur Gourdet, the best greengrocer in Moissac, where my grandmother would spend a whole hour choosing the freshest vegetables, fussing over small details, sniffing, observing. Going to the market was like a trip to the museum—each artichoke was a sculpture to be admired. Then we'd have our little moments in the early evenings, just the two of us, peeling away the artichoke leaves and dipping them in her signature vinaigrette, until we reached the best part, the heart. That's when she would say, "You have it, *chérie*; you're so thin." My aunt, on the other hand, could take whatever was available and turn it into the most miraculous dishes: fish soup with ruddy-colored rouille, roasted lamb with garlic and flageolets, and an endless repertoire of soups, including my favorite, her fava bean soup. My grandmother was the food philosopher, my aunt the master technician.

While my childhood was filled with food, rarely was I the one in the kitchen helping make it. Later, as a student in Paris and London, I had my signature dishes, a few delicious little things I was proud of and that reflected my tastes, but I always spent more time in restaurants than in my own kitchen. It wasn't until I married and started a family that the kitchen won me over. Yet I feel as if I had been preparing for this role all my life; all the places I've been, all the meals I've had, come together in the pots and pans of my kitchen.

It was an unplanned process that led us to Médoc in the first place. Even now I would be at a loss to explain exactly why we took the plunge. But we needed a bigger place for a growing family, so why not think outside the box, outside Paris? My husband wanted more dogs, we wanted to see the kids running around in a big garden, we were up for an adventure.

The last few years have been a revelation. For a city girl to move to Médoc, one of the more remote and untouched parts of France, was a bit of a shock. I felt somewhat lost the first few months—no hairdresser downstairs, no bakery on the corner. In their place, I have a view of the forest from my bedroom window and, when I am really lucky, a herd of deer roaming my garden in the early hours, so quietly that the dogs don't even notice them. Gone are the classic parquet floors of our apartment in Paris, the rosettes and stately flourish, the marble mantlepieces, the black painted French

balconies, and our tiny kitchen. Now we have beautiful stone floors, rustic walls with real character, fireplaces in every room (which we use for grilling birds in winter), thousands of roses climbing up the wall and decorating one side of the house, and a giant rosemary bush just outside the kitchen window that perfumes the dogs as they pass it by and then bring its scent into the house.

Never have I been so aware of the changing of the seasons, the different pleasures that each of them has to offer. I grow my own vegetables and even some fruits. I've made peace with the moles that dig up our garden. Gradually we have found our favorite everything—from the best baguette to the most perfect duck legs, from where to buy foie gras, to which wines we like best and from what years. We've befriended the winemakers, snail farmers, and hunters who regularly pass by our house (and make our dogs crazy).

I am fascinated by the contrasts of the Médoc region, which boasts pine forests where wild boar roam, endless white beaches along the Atlantic, and some of the most famous vineyards in the world. When I first came here, I was worried that the châteaux had been modernized too much and lost their charm, so I was relieved to find that even if the owners might have brushed up on their techniques, the building façades remain as glorious as ever. Driving up from Bordeaux, through the famous villages of Margaux and Pauillac, is like being in an American movie about France, in the best possible sense. In some ways, Médoc is the anti-Provence, for better and worse—not a souvenir shop in sight, and sometimes, less conveniently, not even a loaf of bread. A peninsula detached from the rest of France, Médoc is unknown to many, even to many French. People have drunk the wine but never seen the châteaux. The locals happily go about their lives, enjoying their isolation from the rest of the world.

A few months after we moved, my daughter Gaïa was born, and a year after that, I launched *Manger*, my food blog. I had been encouraged by friends, houseguests, and family to start one—because of my cooking, because they wanted my recipes, because of the way we live, because my husband is a photographer, because we have so many kids and dogs, because I had the time. So, one night in April, out of the blue, without telling anyone, I wrote my first post. I wasn't sure the world needed another food blog, but I felt I had something to offer: French home cooking in English, from someone who really knows the country—and from an insider who is also an outsider. Being half-French, half-Chinese, I fit in everywhere and nowhere. I grew up in Hong Kong and that place is now partly gone. I've lived in France almost half my life, but I don't consider myself completely French.

I still marvel in my little finds and discoveries, and I wanted to share them, to tell the world about Médoc, to encourage people to take risks and to follow their dreams, whether that means picking up and moving to an old farmhouse in the French countryside or simply trying a new recipe for dinner.

As I am a mother of five and a stepmom to two, children are also high on my list of priorities. My husband, Oddur, and I are (or try to be) serious about educating them about food—from a health perspective, sure, but also in terms of broadening their minds and their palates. We want them to enjoy food as much as we do, and to behave themselves at the table, whether at home or in a restaurant. I love to take them through the whole process of growing vegetables and then cooking them. I want them to understand where food comes from, and how you can transform ingredients in simple ways. And it's paying off. Mia, my ten-year-old, frequently gives our visitors lectures

on nutrition and how to have a healthier life through what you eat. Louise, my five-year-old prima donna, has the most impeccable table manners (when she wants to) but is perhaps a little too sure of what she does and doesn't want on her plate. Hudson, who is seven, is the biggest gourmand of them all. I have never seen him say no to any food—he really is the boy who ate everything. Then we have Gaïa, the two-year-old, who pesters her father every night at the aperitif hour for pickles and charcuterie. Thorir, my sixteen-year-old stepson, arrives here for his holidays with a fantasy menu of what to eat, a list of the things he has to have before he leaves. For him, eating is a competitive sport and his greatest fear is not having enough of everything. Gunnhildur, the eldest, is so polite she will eat anything, even if it's far from her favorite. She's the kindest critic and will be anyone's dream dinner party guest.

Most of my culinary fantasies have come true, because everything they say about the French way of life is true—especially the food part.

Before we left Paris, Oddur and I were lucky enough to work on a special project, a food guide to Paris. We spent eighteen months going to a new restaurant almost every weekday, tasting the food, interviewing the chefs, getting their stories and, most important, some of their secrets. It was fascinating for me, having spent such a great deal of my life in the dining rooms of countless establishments, to find myself on the other side of the wall, in the steamy rooms where the action happens. I listened for hundreds of hours as countless chefs—young and old, famous or just starting out—poured their hearts out and spoke about their philosophy of cooking, their preferences, their purveyors. Ingredients, it turned out, are what almost every good chef in France believes to be the most important thing.

Even as other cities, from Copenhagen to Sydney to Tokyo to San Sebastián, claim to rival or have surpassed the French in the kitchen, France will always have its traditions, opinions, and ingredients. The other day, I was out by the side of the road, picking through the brush, when a truck driver passing by inquired, "Are there any?" He knew I was looking for cèpes without even asking. I showed him the small bounty I had collected in my basket and before I knew it, he had parked his huge truck by the side of the road and jumped out to see if he, too, could find some for himself for dinner.

When we lived in Paris, we had four butchers and five bakers on our little stretch of street, and most of them had lines at certain hours of the day. A trip to a French butcher is not just a simple affair of pointing at the lamb chops and saying, "I want eight of those." On the contrary, it involves a bit of banter; an exchange of recipes, perhaps; a discussion of meals past and present; and an account of how your last purchases worked out. Our little village manages to support two bakeries, despite the fact that some of our neighbors prefer one in the next town—even though it means an extra fifteen minutes in the car.

People take pride in their food and they take it seriously: you tell them your recipe for *blanquette de veau,* they counter with theirs. You start a discussion on the best way to make a foie gras terrine, and you will be told by someone that his family's recipe is the best—but it's a secret and he can't share it. It is not uncommon to hear office workers on their lunch breaks debating the best way to make hot chocolate or whether a certain sauce should have shallots or not. In France, when it comes to food, there is a right way to do everything—but everyone's right way is not the same. Everyone has an opinion and that is, as Inspector Clouseau might say, why France is France.

Although we are people who like to eat, we are accustomed to waiting for seasonal pleasures: strawberries in May and June,

bright red (or yellow) tomatoes in July, mush-rooms in the fall. We want what we want when it's in season. One of my favorite chefs, Alain Passard, says it best: *"Les tomates en Décembre, ce n'est pas normal!"* And then he makes a face that suggests that everyone simply must agree. For the most part, they do. Just as we put our summer dresses in boxes and start looking for the ice skates, so we bid farewell to plum tarts and apricot desserts. It's not really good-bye, though—it's *au revoir*. We'll be seeing them again, but first we have other foods to tend to: pumpkins, beets, apples, pears, game.

It's so much fun to chase the seasons and cook with fleeting ingredients, to embrace every month and the gifts it brings. Why should anyone want to eat the same things week in week out when every season offers new discoveries and endless possibilities? If I can inspire peo-ple to cook good food with high-quality ingre-dients, using simple everyday French recipes, I will have achieved something. If I can make someone feel that we can all, at some point, live our dreams one way or another, change our lives if we wish to, even if it's just to try it out, then so much the better.

SPRING

My father is an impatient man. He loves eating out in fine French restaurants—it's just the waiting part he can't handle. I have memories of him excusing himself from the table, on one pretense or another, just after we had placed an elaborate order, one he knew would take the kitchen an eternity to cook. He would slip out for a quick bowl of noodles at a Chinese restaurant nearby, arriving back just in time for "dinner," as if nothing had happened. This used to drive my mother crazy, especially because he never admitted where he'd been. I am his daughter and seem to have inherited this impatience; waiting is something I am very bad at, especially when it comes to . . . everything.

I love summer, perhaps because I grew up in a tropical climate, and almost as soon as it has faded away, I can't wait for it to come again. Autumn is exciting and beautiful; winter can be comforting and is, of course, crowned by the biggest feast of all, Christmas. But by spring, my patience is all but running out. I long for warmer days, light dresses, afternoon swims, and fresh fruits and vegetables. And I yearn for beautiful flowers. Adding to all this, my birthday is at the end of March, and I don't think I need to tell you how bad I am at waiting for my party and presents. Nature must think this impatience is funny, because twice I have been due to give birth in spring and both of those babies made me wait longer than expected.

But waiting breeds anticipation and intense gratefulness. I greet every tulip and daffodil with a song in my heart. The season starts slowly, with a few buds, a handful of crocuses popping up from the soil, but it ends in a full-blown symphony of flowers, cherry blossoms, apple trees, and, the queen of them all, magnolias. In many ways, magnolias are spring to me. When I lived in Paris, I would go to the Palais Royal gardens almost every day in March to see if the magnolia trees had blossomed. If they had, it meant that summer was near; if not, my heart would sink a bit, but then I might cheer myself up by going to a nearby restaurant for lunch. In Paris, we were so spoiled with choices, seemingly endless options, each place better than the next.

In Médoc, we have many magnolia trees but fewer restaurants, which is why we tend to have most meals at home. Seasonal cooking is one of life's greatest joys; it may present a challenge, but the rewards are ample. Most of the year, nature fills my pantry with an abundance of ingredients, empowering me in the kitchen, making me feel invincible at the stove. But spring is a tricky period. From a culinary perspective, nature hasn't started giving. Fruits are still little flowers and the strawberries of May seem an eternity away. The big hearty stews of winter that felt so comforting at Christmas are now clashing with my impatient heart, already fantasizing about swimsuits and parasols.

So what is a cook to do? In early spring, I look to my old friends, the onions and the eggs, to carry me through until nature obliges. Confits and canelés tide me over. And finally, with a little bit of patience and luck, the glorious day arrives when someone has fresh asparagus at the market, a handful of fava beans. Then come the artichokes, and before I know it, I'm once more on that food carousel that will take me through summer and into the bounties of fall—until I find myself back in March, waiting for it all to begin again.

STARTERS

My Aunt Francine's Fava Bean Soup

Watercress Velouté

Artichoke Tartlets

Onion Tart

Artichoke Soufflé

Roast Asparagus with Chervil

Chou Farçi

MAIN COURSES

Lobster with Jura Wine Sauce

Parisian Sole

Roast Chicken with Crème Fraîche and Herbs

Pan-Seared Chicken Breasts with Spring Onions

Duck Confit Parmentier

Roast Lamb Shoulder with Garlic Cream Sauce

Aniseed Sweetbreads with Glazed Turnips

DESSERTS

Gâteau Basque

Garden Cake

Canelés de Bordeaux

Bugnes with Orange Flower Water

Black Locust Flower Fritters

Sugared-Almond Tart

MY AUNT FRANCINE'S
FAVA BEAN SOUP

My aunt is a wonderful cook and I spent a big part of my summers as a child watching her cook in her kitchen in the south of France. Like my grandmother, she's always been a bit ahead of her time in terms of healthy eating, championing seasonal cooking long before it became fashionable. This soup is the recipe I most associate with her. It's mainly made of vegetables, is delicious and healthy, and has a few little gourmet touches, including the unexpected garnishes hidden in the soup (bits of pancetta and croutons). I make this all the time in spring, and luckily for me I have an army of kids to shell the fava beans.

START THE SOUP. Snap off a tip of each pod and squeeze out the beans. Peel the outer layer off each fava bean and discard.

In a large pot, heat the olive oil over medium heat and cook the onion until translucent, about 4 to 5 minutes. Add the fava beans, garlic, and potato, season with salt and pepper, and stir for a couple of minutes. Pour in the stock and enough water to cover the vegetables; season again with salt and pepper. Bring to a boil, then lower the heat and simmer until the potato is cooked through, 20 to 25 minutes.

Meanwhile, prepare the garnishes. Preheat the oven to 350°F/180°C.

Fry the pancetta in a sauté pan over medium heat until golden and crisp. Scoop out with a spoon and drain on a paper towel.

(recipe continues)

SERVES 4

For the soup

1 pound / 450 g shelled large fava beans (from 4 pounds / 1.8 kg in the shell; see Note)

2 tablespoons extra-virgin olive oil

1 onion, sliced

3 garlic cloves, sliced

1 large potato, peeled and diced

Fine sea salt and freshly ground black pepper

⅓ cup / 80 ml chicken or vegetable stock

For the garnishes

5 thin slices pancetta

½ stale baguette, sliced

1 garlic clove, cut in half

¼ cup / 60 ml extra-virgin olive oil

Fine sea salt and freshly ground black pepper

½ cup / 120 ml mascarpone

A large handful of fresh mint leaves, finely chopped

2 shallots, minced

A pinch of piment d'Espelette (optional)

Rub the bread with the garlic clove and drizzle with the olive oil. Season with salt and pepper. Set on a parchment-paper-lined baking sheet and toast in the oven until golden and crisp, about 10 minutes. Set the croûtons aside to cool.

Chop the pancetta and croûtons separately into little bits (you can use a food processor, if you'd like).

In a small bowl, whisk the mascarpone with 2 tablespoons of the chopped mint.

When the soup is done, purée it, in batches if need be, in a food processor or blender and return it to the pot. Reheat the soup over low heat for a few minutes, then season to taste.

To serve, scoop a little of the shallots, remaining mint, the croûtons, and pancetta into the bottom of each bowl. Pour in the hot soup and top each serving with a scoop of the mascarpone. Sprinkle lightly with piment d'Espelette, if desired. Serve immediately.

NOTE: *In France, at the market you have a choice between regular fava beans and larger ones for soups (*fèves pour soupes*). They are extra-large and easy to peel without blanching. With smaller ones, I usually blanch them quickly in boiling water first so they are easier to peel.*

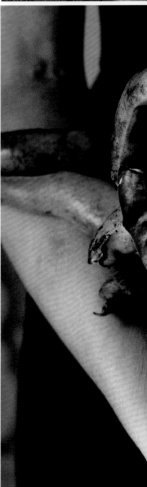

WATERCRESS VELOUTÉ

This recipe works like magic. I enjoy watching the leaves quickly melt away, turning into a delicious and rewarding soup, one that's slightly bitter and so tasty. It's a perfect meal on a relaxing Sunday night. Serve, if you like, with toasts topped with melted cheese. And a glass of crisp white wine!

POUR THE CHICKEN STOCK into a saucepan and bring to a boil.

Meanwhile, in a large saucepan, heat the olive oil over medium heat. Add the shallots and cook until soft, about 4 minutes. Add the watercress, season with salt and pepper, and stir to wilt. Add the potatoes and hot stock, bring to a boil, and cook for 2 minutes. Lower the heat and simmer until the potatoes are tender, about 8 minutes.

Purée the soup in a blender until smooth. Stir in the butter until melted and season to taste with salt and pepper.

Ladle the soup into bowls and top each with a spoonful of crème fraîche and some chives. Serve immediately.

SERVES 4

2 cups / 475 ml chicken or vegetable stock

2 tablespoons extra-virgin olive oil

2 shallots, finely chopped

2 bunches watercress, chopped (including tender stems)

Fine sea salt and freshly ground black pepper

2 medium russet potatoes, peeled and thinly sliced (I use a mandoline)

2 tablespoons / 30 g unsalted butter

⅓ cup / 80 ml crème fraîche

2 tablespoons finely chopped fresh chives

ARTICHOKE TARTLETS

I am very fond of savory tarts and love to have them for little snacks or small meals (with a good glass of wine) or to serve them as starters ahead of meat or fish. I think my favorite such tart is this one, made with baby artichokes sautéed in butter with shallots. Baby artichokes are so lovely to cook with and arranging them in the tartlet shells feels like making beautiful edible bouquets.

ON A LIGHTLY FLOURED SURFACE, roll out the dough ¼ inch/0.5 cm thick. Cut out 6 rounds large enough to line six tartlet molds, each about 3 inches/7.5 cm in diameter. (Alternatively, you can simply cut disks of the same size and skip the molds.) Put the rounds on a baking sheet and refrigerate for 30 minutes.

Preheat the oven to 350°F/180°C.

Fill a large bowl with cold water and squeeze the juice from the lemons into it. Rinse the artichokes. Working with one at a time and putting them in the lemon water as you go, trim the stems to ¼ inch/6 mm from the base. Peel back and remove the outer petals until the pale green leaves appear. Cut off the sharp tips. Trim off any remaining green from the base of the artichokes. Halve or quarter the artichokes, depending upon size, and return to the lemon water to prevent browning.

Drain the artichokes and pat dry. In a large sauté pan, heat the olive oil over medium heat. Sauté the artichokes and shallots until slightly golden, 4 to 5 minutes. Add the sprigs of thyme and season with salt and pepper. Lower the heat, cover with a lid, and continue cooking until the artichokes are tender, 10 to 12 minutes. Remove from the heat and let cool for 10 minutes. Discard the thyme.

(recipe continues)

8 ounces/230 g puff pastry, homemade (recipe follows) or store-bought

2 lemons, halved

12 baby artichokes

⅓ cup/80 ml extra-virgin olive oil, plus more for drizzling

4 shallots, minced

A few sprigs of fresh thyme

Fine sea salt and freshly ground black pepper

½ bunch fresh parsley, leaves removed and finely chopped

Meanwhile, line the molds with the pastry and prick the bases with a fork. Line with parchment paper and pie weights or dried beans and bake for 8 minutes. Remove the parchment paper and weights and bake until golden, another 5 minutes or so. (If you are not using molds, cover the disks with parchment paper and another baking sheet and bake for 8 minutes, then remove the baking sheet and bake for another 5 minutes.)

Scoop 1 tablespoon of shallots into each tartlet shell and arrange a few artichokes on top. Drizzle with olive oil. Bake for 5 minutes, or until the pastry is golden and crisp. Drizzle with a little bit more olive oil and sprinkle with the parsley before serving.

PUFF PASTRY
(PÂTE FEUILLETÉE)

By following these instructions, you will be able to produce delicious home-made puff pastry.

IN A LARGE BOWL, mix the flour and salt. Cube 4 tablespoons/50 g of the butter and add to the bowl, along with the water. Mix gently with your fingertips until the dough comes together in a ball. Slice a cross in the top of the ball, about ½ inch/2 cm deep. (This will help when rolling the dough.) Wrap in plastic wrap and refrigerate for 30 minutes.

Put the remaining 8 ounces/250 g butter on a piece of plastic wrap, cover with a second sheet, and use a rolling pin to flatten the butter into a 5- to 6-inch/14- to 15-cm square. Chill in the refrigerator for 30 minutes.

MAKES ABOUT 1 POUND
5 OUNCES/600 G

2 cups/240 g all-purpose flour, sifted, plus more for rolling

½ teaspoon fine sea salt

½ cup/120 ml room-temperature water

10 ounces/2½ sticks/300 g unsalted butter, at room temperature

On a lightly floured surface, roll the dough from the center out, following the lines of the cross, as if you were opening the ball like a flower, into a large square, 9 to 10 inches/25 to 30 cm on each side.

Put the flattened butter in the center of the square of dough and bring the corners of the dough to the center to enclose the butter. Roll out, being careful not to squeeze out the butter, to an even rectangular shape about 8 by 12 inches/20 by 30 cm.

With a short side facing you, fold the dough in thirds, as if you were folding a letter. Turn the folded dough so that the seam is to one side and a short side of the dough is once again facing you. Repeat the rolling and folding once. Wrap in plastic wrap and let rest for 30 minutes in the refrigerator.

Repeat the rolling, folding, and chilling steps 4 more times. The idea is to fold and roll the dough six times (twice at the beginning and then once each subsequent time). When you are finished, your dough is ready! You can use it right away or wrap it in plastic wrap and refrigerate it for up to 3 days or freeze it for up to 1 month; defrost overnight in the refrigerator before rolling.

ONION TART

I always have a big bowl of onions on my kitchen table in various shades and sizes. To me they are as beautiful as any vase of flowers and as necessary as running water or a working stove. A friend once asked what I would do if there were no onions—I had no answer then and still don't. They are the eggs of the vegetable world, endlessly versatile, and can be bit players in big dishes or leading stars in French classics like onion soup.

This simple yet flavorful tart is exactly the sort of food I like to have by myself in a bistro when people have started leaving and it's too late to order anything more serious.

HEAT THE OLIVE OIL and butter in a large sauté pan over medium-high heat. Add the bacon and fry until browned, about 3 minutes. Lower the heat to medium-low, add the onions, season with salt and pepper, and cook, stirring occasionally, until tender and golden brown, about 15 minutes.

Add the honey, balsamic vinegar, and thyme, increase the heat to high, and boil to reduce for 2 to 3 minutes. Take off the heat and set aside to cool.

Preheat the oven 400°F/200°C.

On a lightly floured surface, roll out the dough ⅛ inch/0.3 cm thick. Line a 10-inch/25-cm tart pan with the pastry and prick the bottom several times with a fork. Trim the edges. Scoop the onion mixture into the tart shell. Bake until the pastry is crisp and golden, about 20 minutes. Let cool for 5 minutes before drizzling with olive oil and serving.

3 tablespoons extra-virgin olive oil, plus more for drizzling

2 tablespoons unsalted butter

3½ ounces/100 g bacon, cut into lardons or diced

1 pound/450 g onions, thinly sliced

Fine sea salt and freshly ground black pepper

1 tablespoon honey

1 tablespoon balsamic vinegar

A few sprigs of fresh thyme

All-purpose flour for rolling the dough

8 ounces/230 g puff pastry, homemade (page 28) or store-bought

ARTICHOKE SOUFFLÉ

I have a penchant for soufflés and while I usually prefer them sweet, for dessert, I sometimes make savory ones, often with cheese, for an elegant light lunch or a starter. While a nice quiche would serve a similar purpose, a soufflé is so much more fun. In spring, when artichokes start popping up at markets, I always start by having a few of them in the simplest manner, steamed, with vinaigrette. But then one day on a whim I had the idea to mix them into a soufflé, and it worked so well that it's become a springtime favorite. Now we celebrate the arrival of artichokes, and the arrival of spring, with this soufflé.

BRING A LARGE POT of salted water to a boil. Trim the stems from the artichokes.

Cook the artichokes in the boiling water until tender when pierced with a small knife, 45 minutes to an hour, depending on size. Drain and let cool for 10 minutes.

Remove all the leaves and fuzzy chokes from the artichokes and reserve the hearts (the meaty center). Purée the artichoke hearts in a food processor until smooth, 1 to 2 minutes.

Melt the butter in a medium saucepan over medium heat. Add flour and whisk until bubbling and smooth. Gradually add the milk, whisking away. Season with salt and pepper and simmer, still whisking, until the sauce thickens, 8 to 10 minutes. Off the heat, add the Gruyère and whisk until melted. Transfer the béchamel sauce to a bowl and let cool for 10 minutes.

(recipe continues)

4 large artichokes

4 tablespoons / 60 g unsalted butter, plus more for the ramekins

¼ cup / 30 g all-purpose flour, plus more for the ramekins

1 cup / 250 ml whole milk

Fine sea salt and freshly ground black pepper

¼ cup / 25 g grated Gruyère or Comté cheese

4 large eggs, separated

Preheat the oven to 350°F/180°C. Grease four 7-ounce/210-ml ramekins with butter and dust with flour. Tap out the excess flour.

Whisk the egg yolks one by one into the béchamel sauce, then add the artichoke purée, mixing until smooth.

Whisk the egg whites in a large bowl until foamy. (You can use an electric mixer if you like.) Add a pinch of salt and continue whisking until stiff. Fold the egg whites gently into the artichoke mixture. Fill the ramekins to ½ inch/1.2 cm from the top with the soufflé mixture.

Bake until risen and golden, 25 to 30 minutes. Serve immediately.

ROAST ASPARAGUS
with CHERVIL

In April, all of France (and most of Europe) goes crazy for asparagus. For a precious month, everybody tries to get their hands on as much as they can, and no matter where you go, you will be served asparagus. Here in the Bordeaux region, the white variety is most popular. I like to serve the spears with a simple vinaigrette and a poached egg, but my favorite asparagus recipe is this starter: delicate green asparagus wrapped in Bayonne ham and sprinkled with chervil and Parmesan. If I have dinner guests on short notice, I often fall back on this uncomplicated dish.

PREHEAT THE OVEN to 400°F/200°C.

Trim away the bottom third of each asparagus stalk. If the asparagus are on the thick side, peel the stalks with a vegetable peeler. Wrap 4 to 5, depending on size stalks in a slice of the ham and secure with a toothpick. Repeat with the rest of the asparagus and ham.

Put the asparagus on a baking sheet, leaving a little room between the bundles. Season with salt and pepper and drizzle with olive oil. Roast until the ham and asparagus are browned and the asparagus is tender, about 30 minutes.

Just before serving, sprinkle the chervil and some Parmesan shavings over the asparagus.

SERVES 6

1 pound / 450 g asparagus

6 slices Bayonne ham or prosciutto

Fine sea salt and freshly ground black pepper

Extra-virgin olive oil for drizzling

A bunch of fresh chervil, leaves removed and coarsely chopped

Parmesan shavings

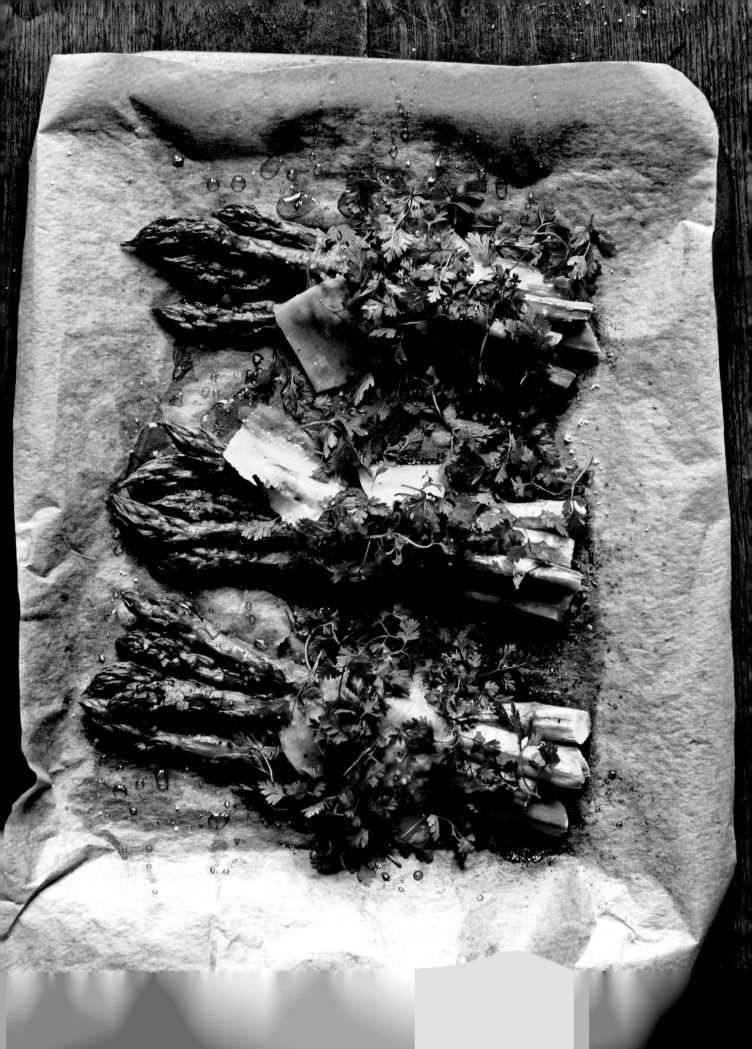

CHOU FARÇI

One of my favorite things to serve alongside meat is braised Savoy cabbage. Wonderful things happen when you cook this bitter vegetable with butter and let all its flavor come out. This little dish is a variation on serving meat with cabbage—it's all wrapped together in a pretty parcel. Serve it on its own, as a weekend lunch, or as an appetizer for a decadent feast. It's the sort of dish that will make those at your table wonder, "If this is the starter, what are we having for the main course?"

SERVES 6

1 head Savoy cabbage

Unsalted butter for the pan

2 tablespoons extra-virgin olive oil

1 onion, thinly sliced

2 carrots, finely diced

⅔ pound / 300 g ground beef

⅔ pound / 300 g good-quality bulk pork sausage

2 garlic cloves, thinly sliced

2 to 3 sprigs of fresh thyme

1 bay leaf

½ teaspoon Rabelais spice (see Note) or ground allspice

Fine sea salt and freshly ground black pepper

¾ cup / 100 g canned whole tomatoes, crushed, with their juices

1 large egg

BRING A LARGE POT of salted water to a boil. Meanwhile, core the cabbage leaves and separate them, discarding any coarse outer ones. Cook the leaves in the boiling water for 8 minutes. Drain and set aside to cool.

Grease the bottom and sides of a 7-inch / 18-cm soufflé dish or charlotte mold with butter. Put a large pretty cabbage leaf, domed side down, in the dish. Top with another leaf and continue arranging the leaves one on top of another until the entire base and sides are covered. You won't use all of the leaves at this point (reserve enough for 4 or 5 layers).

Heat the olive oil in a large sauté pan over medium heat. Cook the onion and carrots until softened, 4 minutes. Add the ground beef, sausage, garlic, thyme, bay leaf, spice, and salt and pepper to taste and cook, stirring once or twice, until the meat is browned.

Pour in the crushed tomatoes, with their juices, and simmer until nearly all the liquid has been absorbed, about 5 minutes. Transfer the mixture to a bowl and let cool.

(recipe continues)

Preheat the oven to 350°F / 180°C.

When the meat mixture has cooled, discard the thyme and bay leaf. Add the egg and mix well.

Put a layer about ½ inch / 1 cm thick of the meat in the cabbage-lined dish and top with a cabbage leaf. Repeat until you've used all of the meat and filled the dish, about 4 layers. Finish with a final layer of cabbage, making sure to tuck in the leaves on all sides.

Bake for 40 minutes. To unmold, invert a plate over the soufflé dish, flip the plate and dish, and remove the mold. Serve immediately, cut into slices.

NOTE: *Rabelais spice is a mix of allspice, nutmeg, and curry—a traditional spice in France since 1820.*

LOBSTER *with*
JURA WINE SAUCE

If I could, I would have lobster every day. I have long admired the beauty and grandeur of these crustaceans; no wonder they are so suited for special occasions. Lobster meat is simply delicious as is, but I love combining the deep, strong taste of Jura wine, or *vin jaune*, with tangy sorrel leaves to bring out the sweetness of the lobster. This dish is a textbook example of taking something already great and finding a way to make it even better.

FILL A LARGE POT with enough salted water to cover the lobsters. Add the bay leaf and bouquet garni and bring to a boil over high heat. Plunge each lobster headfirst into the water, cover the pot, and return to a boil. (You may need to do this in two batches, depending upon the size of your pot.) Reduce the heat and simmer for 15 to 20 minutes, depending on the size of the lobsters. The shells should be bright red and the meat opaque.

Meanwhile, in a saucepan, combine the shallots, wine, and vinegar, season with salt and pepper, and bring to a simmer over medium heat. Simmer until reduced by three quarters, 4 to 5 minutes. Add the butter all at once to the saucepan, reduce the heat, and whisk until blended and the sauce has thickened. Remove from the heat.

Lift the lobsters from the water with kitchen tongs, put them on a large cutting board, and let cool for a few minutes. With a big sharp knife, split each lobster lengthwise in half. Transfer to large plates.

Sprinkle the sorrel into the sauce and pour over the lobsters. Serve immediately.

1 bay leaf

1 bouquet garni (see page 159)

4 live lobsters, 1 to 1½ pounds / 450 to 680 g each

4 shallots, minced

½ cup / 120 ml Jura wine (*vin jaune*) or dry sherry

2 tablespoons white wine vinegar

Fine sea salt and freshly ground black pepper

10 ounces / 2½ sticks / 300 g salted butter, cubed, at room temperature (see Note)

2 bunches sorrel, coarsely chopped

NOTE: *I usually prefer unsalted butter; this is one of the rare exceptions. If you only have unsalted butter, be sure to season the sauce amply with salt.*

PARISIAN SOLE

One of the things I love most about Paris is its old-fashioned restaurants, drenched in history and blessed by charm—the sort of places that have had the same waiters for forty years and serve the same food from one generation to the next. Of course, this only works if the food is any good, but I know more than a dozen restaurants that fit that very description. At such an establishment, I might be tempted to go for calves' kidneys or simply a juicy entrecôte with Béarnaise sauce and fries. But if they had sole with a creamy sauce, I don't think I could resist ordering it, with a glass of crisp dry white wine. Then I'd probably have wild strawberries with crème fraîche for dessert.

HEAT THE OLIVE OIL and 4 tablespoons/60 g of the butter in a large sauté pan over medium heat. Season the sole with salt and pepper and dust lightly with flour. Cook the fillets until golden, 3 to 4 minutes on each side. Transfer to plates and keep warm.

Scrape off and discard any browned bits from the pan. Then add the remaining 2 tablespoons/30 g butter and cook the shallots over medium heat until soft, about 5 minutes. Add the wine and simmer to reduce for 3 minutes. Lower the heat, pour in the cream, and bring to a simmer. Season with salt and pepper.

Pour the sauce over the sole, sprinkle with the parsley, and serve immediately.

SERVES 4

2 tablespoons extra-virgin olive oil

6 tablespoons/90 g unsalted butter

4 sole fillets, 4 ounces/115 g each

Fine sea salt and freshly ground black pepper

All-purpose flour for dusting

5 shallots, thinly sliced

3 tablespoons dry white wine

⅓ cup/80 ml heavy cream

A bunch of fresh parsley, leaves removed and chopped

ROAST CHICKEN *with* CRÈME FRAÎCHE *and* HERBS

Roast chicken is very much a usual suspect at our dinner table. Throughout the years, my go-to version was somewhat Italian in style, perfumed with olive oil, lemon, and thyme. A few years ago, though, I started experimenting with more "French" ingredients, including crème fraîche and lots of garlic. The experiment has been nothing short of a success story and this recipe has dethroned the other version to become our most wanted chicken dish. In fact, it's probably the recipe that dinner guests ask for most often. I once had a guest whose face lit up when he took his first bite and he said, "When I had the glass of Lillet I was pretty sure I was in France, but now that I've had this chicken, I know I couldn't be anywhere else." I guess that's a compliment, right?

PREHEAT THE OVEN to 350°F/180°C.

In a small bowl, mix the crème fraîche, garlic, shallot, parsley, and thyme. Season with fine sea salt and pepper. Spoon half of the mixture inside the cavity of the chicken. Truss the chicken securely with kitchen twine. Rub the remaining cream in a thick layer all over the chicken (make sure to rub under the thighs and wings). Sprinkle the coarse salt over the chicken and put it in a roasting pan.

Roast the chicken until golden brown and cooked through (the juices should run clear, not pink, when you prick the thigh with a knife), about 1 hour. Check the pan halfway through the cooking and add a few tablespoons water, or more if needed, if the bottom of the pan has started to dry out.

Let the chicken rest for 15 minutes before serving.

SERVES 4

1¼ cups / 300 ml crème fraîche

4 garlic cloves, thinly sliced

1 shallot, thinly sliced

A large bunch of fresh parsley, leaves removed and chopped

A few sprigs of fresh thyme

Fine sea salt and freshly ground black pepper

1 whole chicken (3 pounds / 1.3 kg)

½ teaspoon coarse sea salt

PAN-SEARED CHICKEN BREASTS *with* SPRING ONIONS

This is a simple and delicious dish I am in love with. But, as we all know, sometimes the simplest things are the hardest to master. The success of cooking this chicken to perfection rests on two things: the quality of the products and the alchemy of the Jura wine. It's inspired by various chicken dishes that I've had, both in France and Hong Kong, where they like to cook chicken with fermented rice wine, which has a somewhat similar effect. The chicken breasts should have a thick layer of fatty skin and be seared so that the outside is crispy but the inside remains moist. Jura wine, which tastes like a mixture of sherry and white wine, adds a flavor unlike any other and is a real pleasure to cook with. (If you can't find Jura wine, then dry sherry is a decent substitute.) Talking about divine pairings, when I cook with this golden wine, I always make sure to leave a bit for myself as a treat so I can enjoy it later with some walnuts and Comté cheese. I call it the chef's privilege.

PREHEAT THE OVEN to 325°F/160°C.

Drizzle the olive oil over the chicken breasts and season with salt and pepper. Heat a large heavy sauté pan over high heat. Add the chicken breasts skin side down; the high heat of the pan and oil will turn the skin crisp and golden. Once the skin is golden, after about 4 minutes, turn the chicken and brown on the other side, about 2 minutes.

Transfer to a baking sheet (set the pan aside) and finish cooking in the oven, about 8 minutes.

4 skin-on, boneless chicken breast halves

2 tablespoons extra-virgin olive oil for drizzling

Fine sea salt and freshly ground black pepper

8 spring onions (including stalks), split lengthwise

3 tablespoons unsalted butter

3 tablespoons chicken stock

6 tablespoons/100 ml Jura wine (*vin joune*) or dry sherry

A small bunch of fresh chives, finely chopped

Meanwhile, add the spring onions to the fat remaining in the sauté pan and cook over high heat until the stalks are slightly crisp, about 3 minutes on each side. Transfer to the baking sheet with the chicken.

Melt 2 tablespoons of the butter in the pan and then scrape up the browned bits from the bottom of the pan. Add the chicken stock and simmer over high heat to reduce it for a few minutes, and then add the wine and the remaining 1 tablespoon butter. Season with salt and pepper and stir until the sauce has thickened, 3 to 4 minutes.

Serve the chicken breasts with the spring onions, drizzle the wine sauce on top, and sprinkle with the chives.

DUCK CONFIT
PARMENTIER

DUCK CONFIT PARMENTIER

Confit de canard has become something of a cliché: It's standard on most bistro menus in France and in French restaurants around the world and you can even buy it canned in most supermarkets. But when it's good, it exemplifies in one bite what French cooking is all about: beautiful ingredients cooked in a traditional, often simple way. I like to serve this national dish to guests in its purest form, accompanied by roast potatoes and mustard. It's always a hit.

As good as duck confit is, sometimes I like to take it one step further toward culinary nirvana and turn it into a Parmentier, or shepherd's pie. That, of course, is another classic, but I find good versions of it hard to come by in restaurants. It's usually decent enough but rarely breathtaking—and believe me, this dish can be breathtaking.

This Parmentier is only as good as the *confit de canard* you start with (whether you make it yourself or not), and the most important thing is to keep it moist and use a decent wine for the cooking. Serve with a crisp green salad on the side.

PREHEAT THE OVEN to 350°F/180°C.

Make the duck layer. Remove the skin and bones from the duck legs and shred the meat into bite-sized pieces.

In a large sauté pan, cook the onion, shallots, and garlic in the butter over medium heat until tender and slightly golden, 4 to 5 minutes. Add the duck meat and parsley and cook for 2 more minutes. Pour in the wine and simmer to reduce for 4 to 5 minutes. Transfer to a 9 × 13-inch/23 × 33-cm baking dish.

Make the mashed potatoes. Put the potatoes in a pot, cover with salted water, bring to a boil, and cook until tender, about 15 minutes. Drain the

SERVES 4

For the duck

4 duck confit legs, homemade (recipe follows) or store-bought

1 onion, thinly sliced

2 shallots, thinly sliced

2 tablespoons butter

2 garlic cloves, minced

A handful of finely chopped fresh parsley

⅔ cup/160 ml dry red wine

For the mashed potatoes

3 pounds/1.3 to 1.5 kg large russet potatoes (5 to 6), peeled

4 tablespoons unsalted butter, at room temperature

¼ cup/30 ml crème fraîche

Fine sea salt and freshly ground black pepper

⅔ cup/60 g freshly grated Parmesan cheese

potatoes, return to the pot, and mash with the butter and crème fraîche. Season with salt and pepper.

Top the duck mixture with the mashed potatoes. With a fork, flatten the potatoes into an even layer. Sprinkle with the Parmesan.

Bake the Parmentier until golden brown, about 25 minutes.

DUCK CONFIT

SPRINKLE THE DUCK LEGS all over with a generous amount of salt and pepper and rub into the skin and flesh. Put in a baking dish or shallow bowl, cover with plastic wrap, and refrigerate overnight.

Rinse the duck legs under cold running water. Pat dry with a kitchen towel.

In a pot just big enough to hold the legs in a single layer, melt the duck fat. Add the duck legs, bay leaf, garlic, and thyme and cook over medium-low heat at a steady gentle simmer (160° to 175°F/70° to 80°C) until the duck legs are cooked through and golden, about 2 hours.

Transfer the duck legs to a plate and strain the duck fat through a sieve into a wide pan or baking dish, just large enough to hold the legs. Add the duck legs to the fat and let cool. Ideally, there should be a thin layer of fat covering the legs. The duck can be refrigerated for up to 2 weeks.

To serve the legs on their own, in a sauté pan, fry them in the butter until slightly crisp and golden, 3 to 4 minutes on each side. Serve immediately.

SERVES 4

4 medium duck legs

Coarse sea salt and freshly ground black pepper

About 1¼ cups / 300 g rendered duck fat

1 bay leaf

3 garlic cloves

3 sprigs of fresh thyme

3 tablespoons unsalted butter (if panfrying the legs)

ROAST LAMB SHOULDER *with* GARLIC CREAM SAUCE

Easter may be my favorite holiday. It's all about enjoying good food, reflecting, and spending time with family, without any of the gift-giving stress of Christmas. Lamb for Easter is a must—along with chocolate and daffodils. While garlic goes well with almost any type of meat, I think it is never more at home than when married with lamb. I love simple pan-seared lamb chops with caramelized garlic and rosemary or a shoulder of lamb with bread crumbs and garlic.

But for me the most French way of serving lamb is to accompany it with this creamy garlic-infused sauce. Just imagine the treat of scooping up the sauce and meat juices with a piece of good bread at the end of the meal. After this creamy sauce, I love to serve a rich chocolate cake and finish my glass of red wine with the first bites. Then I have coffee with my second serving of cake.

SERVES 6

One 3-pound / 1.3-kg bone-in lamb shoulder

Fine sea salt and freshly ground pepper

A large bunch of fresh rosemary

6 large garlic heads

Extra-virgin olive oil for drizzling

¾ cup / 180 ml heavy cream

⅓ cup / 80 ml whole milk

1 tablespoon cornstarch

PREHEAT THE OVEN to 300°F / 150°C.

Put the lamb shoulder in a large roasting pan. Score the fat in a crosshatch pattern at ½-inch / 1.5-cm intervals. Season generously with salt and pepper. Slip half the rosemary sprigs under the lamb and put the other half on top. Slice 5 of the garlic heads horizontally in half and scatter around the lamb. Drizzle the meat and garlic with olive oil. Cover the pan tightly with aluminum foil.

Transfer the pan to the oven and roast the lamb for about 5 hours, until the meat is very tender; it should pull apart when you stick a fork into it.

(recipe continues)

Meanwhile, about ½ hour before the meat is ready, separate the remaining head of garlic into cloves; peel 10 cloves (reserve the rest for another use). Combine the garlic, cream, and milk in a small saucepan and simmer over medium-low heat until the garlic is very soft and the mixture has thickened, 20 to 25 minutes.

Off the heat, whisk in the cornstarch, ⅓ cup/80 ml of the juices from the roasting pan (avoid the fat that rises to the top), and a pinch of salt. Still whisking, return to the heat and let the sauce simmer until it is thick enough to coat a spoon, about 2 minutes. Strain the sauce through a sieve.

Let the meat rest for 15 minutes before serving.

The lamb will easily pull apart into pieces. Serve with the sauce on the side.

ANISESEED SWEETBREADS
with GLAZED TURNIPS

For a long time, sweetbreads were on the list of things that I simply didn't like. I'd had them from time to time and mostly been unimpressed. But they are my husband's favorite food, and when we lived in Paris, he always had them on his birthday. After we moved to Médoc, we found restaurants with sweetbreads harder to come by, so I started to make them at home as a once-a-year treat. Sweetbreads sound like such a complicated thing to make, but aside from the overnight soaking, they are actually quick and easy to cook. I like to sauté them with aniseed and serve them with a wine and shallot sauce. I don't know if it's the aniseed or just the fact that I've now cooked them many times, but I must say I have started to like sweetbreads a lot, especially served with a tasty celery root mash or, even better, glazed turnips, as here.

SOAK THE SWEETBREADS. Put the sweetbreads in a bowl and cover with water mixed with 1 tablespoon of the coarse salt. Refrigerate overnight.

Drain the sweetbreads. Pull off and discard the outer membranes and any veins. Rinse and put in a medium pot. Cover with water, add the remaining 1 tablespoon coarse salt, and bring to a boil. Remove from the heat and leave the sweetbreads in the water for 15 minutes.

Drain the sweetbreads and plunge them into a bowl of ice-cold water until cool, then drain again and pat dry. Slice into small medallions, about ½ inch / 1.5 cm thick. Season with salt and pepper and sprinkle with the aniseed. Set aside.

(recipe continues)

For the sweetbreads

12 ounces / 340 g veal sweetbreads

2 tablespoons coarse sea salt

Fine sea salt and freshly ground black pepper

1 teaspoon aniseed

3 tablespoons unsalted butter

2 tablespoons extra-virgin olive oil

For the sauce

2 teaspoons unsalted butter

2 shallots, thinly sliced

½ cup / 120 ml dry white wine

Fine sea salt and freshly ground black pepper

3 tablespoons beef stock

Glazed Turnips (recipe follows)

Make the sauce. Melt 1 teaspoon of the butter in a small sauté pan over medium heat. Add the shallots and cook until soft, 4 minutes. Pour in the wine and simmer to reduce by half. Season with salt and pepper. Add the stock and the remaining 1 teaspoon butter and cook until the sauce is glossy, about 2 minutes. Strain the sauce through a sieve into a bowl or small saucepan; keep warm.

Cook the sweetbreads. Heat the butter and olive oil in a large sauté pan over high heat. Add the sweetbreads and cook until golden and crisp, about 4 minutes on each side.

Arrange the sweetbreads on serving plates and drizzle with the wine sauce. Serve immediately, with the glazed turnips.

GLAZED TURNIPS

CUT THE STEMS and leaves from the turnips, leaving a bit of green on top. If the skin is tender, there is no need to peel the turnips; if they are larger, peel them.

In a large saucepan, melt the butter over medium heat. Add the turnips and stir to coat with the butter. Season with salt and pepper. Add the stock, wine, and sugar, increase the heat, and bring to a boil. Reduce the heat to low, cover the pan, and simmer gently, stirring occasionally, until the sauce has lightly caramelized and the turnips are tender, 20 minutes. Season to taste.

Sprinkle with the parsley just before serving.

SERVES 2

1 pound / 450 g small to medium baby turnips

1½ tablespoons unsalted butter

Fine sea salt and freshly ground black pepper

¾ cup / 180 ml beef or vegetable stock

2 tablespoons dry white wine

1½ tablespoons granulated sugar

1 tablespoon finely chopped fresh parsley

SPRING FEAST

ONION TART 30

DUCK CONFIT
PARMENTIER 52

BUGNES WITH
ORANGE FLOWER
WATER 73

I love the early days of spring,

when mornings are blue and

bright, when days are still chilly

and sometimes wet. It's the time

of year when I need heartwarming

dishes, the jams and onions and jars

of duck—treasures that can always be

found in my pantry, even after

a long, hard winter.

GÂTEAU BASQUE

One way to judge a restaurant is to order a classic dessert, like rice pudding or gâteau Basque, and see how much effort they have put into it. Just because the steak was delicious or the decor lovely doesn't mean that they can just give you any old dessert or cake! The simplest dishes often tell the most striking stories.

This Basque cake is at once rustic and traditional but also light, silky, and wonderfully tasty. There are several versions, with vanilla (or sometimes rum-flavored) pastry cream or cherry jam fillings; I prefer the ones with pastry cream. This is a modest-looking dessert but very satisfying, especially when you want a sweet that is a little *gourmand*.

PREPARE THE CREAM FILLING. In a medium saucepan, bring the milk and vanilla seeds to a low boil over medium-low heat. Add the sugar and whisk for 30 seconds. Gradually add the flour, whisking away for 2 minutes to prevent any lumps. You can take the saucepan on and off the heat a few times if you are afraid of scorching the mixture. Reduce the heat to low and add the egg and egg yolks one at a time, still whisking away. Then whisk until the mixture has thickened, 2 to 3 minutes. Remove from the heat, add the rum, and mix well.

Press a piece of plastic wrap against the surface to prevent it from forming a skin and set aside to cool completely. Then refrigerate for at least 4 hours, or overnight.

Meanwhile, make the dough. In a large bowl, mix the sugar and butter with a wooden spoon until smooth. Gradually add the eggs and egg yolks, mixing until the dough is smooth. Add the flour, salt, and baking powder

(recipe continues)

For the cream filling

2 cups / 475 ml whole milk

1 vanilla bean, split lengthwise, seeds scraped out and reserved

½ cup / 100 g granulated sugar

½ cup / 50 g all-purpose flour, sifted

1 large egg

2 large egg yolks

2 tablespoons dark rum

For the dough

1 cup / 200 g granulated sugar

13 tablespoons / 200 g unsalted butter, cut into pieces, at room temperature, plus more for the pan

2 large eggs

4 large egg yolks

3⅓ cups / 400 g all-purpose flour, sifted, plus more for rolling and for the pan

½ teaspoon fine sea salt

1 teaspoon baking powder

1 large egg yolk

Pinch of fine sea salt

and mix well; the dough will be soft. Divide the dough in half, shape into 2 balls, and wrap in plastic wrap. Refrigerate for 1 hour.

Preheat the oven to 350°F/180°C. Butter a 9-inch/23-cm round cake pan and dust with flour.

One at a time, roll out each ball of dough on a lightly floured surface (I like to roll it out on floured parchment so it doesn't stick to the counter) into a round, about ½ inch/1.5 cm thick; you want a slightly larger base (about 12 inches/30 cm in diameter) and a slightly smaller top layer (about 9 inches/23 cm in diameter).

Line the cake pan with the larger round of dough, leaving a ¾-inch/2-cm overhang. Pour the cream filling into the pan and cover with the smaller round. Stir together the egg yolk and salt to make an egg wash, brush the overhang of the dough with the egg wash, and press the edges together to seal, folding the overhang up and over. Brush the top with egg wash and use a fork to score lines on the top of the cake (see photo, page 62). Make 3 to 4 tiny incisions in the top with the tip of a sharp knife to release steam.

Bake until the cake is golden brown, about 30 minutes. Cool on a wire rack for at least 40 minutes before serving.

EGGS

I love eggs—so ordinary, yet so well crafted and special. If eggs were man-made, they'd win first prize in every design competition. They are versatile and always appropriate, ready to be cooked on their own in various ways or turned into something delicious, either sweet or savory. My kids love nothing better than *oeufs à la coque* (soft-boiled eggs), my husband goes mad for Béarnaise sauce, and I simply couldn't live without meringues. There is a scene in *Forrest Gump* where his army buddy spends his time recounting all the possible ways of cooking shrimp. That's how I feel about eggs; the possibilities are endless.

GARDEN CAKE

What can I say . . . this is the cake that started it all. One early spring evening, inspired by all the new flowers in the garden, I decided to make a cake on a whim—a typical Icelandic creamy meringue cake, inspired by a recipe from my Icelandic mother-in-law. There was something in the air that night, something fresh and exciting. I wanted this cake to be a celebration of spring, of the garden, something out of a fairy tale. When my garden cake was ready, I posted a picture of it online. Little did I know it would be pinned, tumblrd, linked to on Facebook, and tweeted; it was all over the Internet—and so my blog, *Manger*, was born. It was a gift from spring, and I am forever grateful.

PREHEAT THE OVEN to 275°F/135°C. Line a large baking sheet with parchment paper.

In a large very clean bowl (make sure that there are no traces of grease in it, or the whites will not whip to their fullest), beat the egg whites with an electric mixer on medium speed until they form soft peaks. Still whipping, add the sugar little by little, so it is well dissolved, then whip until the meringue is stiff and glossy.

Using a narrow spatula, form 2 meringues, each 8 inches/20 cm across and 2 inches/5 cm high, on the parchment-lined baking sheet. Bake until the meringues are crisp on top, about 55 minutes. Turn off the oven and leave the meringues in the oven, with the door propped open, for 25 minutes, then transfer to a rack to cool.

Whip the cream until it is light, fluffy, and holds soft peaks. Add the vanilla extract.

(recipe continues)

SERVES 6

6 large egg whites, at room temperature

1¾ cups/350 g superfine sugar

1 cup/250 ml heavy cream

¼ teaspoon vanilla extract

Big handfuls of your favorite berries (I use raspberries, blueberries, and red currants)

Pretty organic/unsprayed edible flowers and leaves of your choice

Spread half of the whipped cream over one of the meringues. Scatter as many berries as you like over the cream and sandwich the other meringue on top, flat side up. Spread the remaining whipped cream on top of the second meringue. Now you can enjoy decorating your cake with berries, leaves, and flowers—all things bright and beautiful. The cake is best eaten immediately.

NOTES: *The flowers and leaves in the photo are* not *edible and were used purely for decorative purposes.*

I don't add sugar to the whipped cream because the meringue is very sweet. If you prefer to sweeten the cream, add ¼ cup / 30 g sifted confectioners' sugar.

CANELÉS DE BORDEAUX

When I lived in Paris, canelés were a little treat that I bought regularly at my local *pâtisserie*. I always enjoyed them with coffee, and I knew they came from Bordeaux but otherwise had not given them much thought. Then we moved to Médoc, and they were *everywhere*. These days I love to have them with wine after dinner. Although the traditional copper molds are much more beautiful and special, I usually use a silicone one for practical reasons; it is so much easier to clean. Canelés should have a caramelized crust and a soft inside, so you and your oven might have to make several attempts before they turn out absolutely perfect.

IN A MEDIUM SAUCEPAN, whisk together the milk and vanilla seeds. Bring to a boil, then remove from the heat and set aside for 5 minutes. Transfer to a bowl.

Whisk in the sugar and flour, trying to avoid lumps (if there are many lumps, simply strain the batter through a sieve). Add the egg yolks one by one, whisking gently to mix. Stir in the butter. Finally, add the rum and whisk the batter until smooth. The batter should be similar to a crêpe batter—not too thick, not too thin. Cover and refrigerate for 24 hours.

Preheat the oven to 450°F/230°C.

Fill 16 canelé molds two-thirds full. Bake for exactly 5 minutes, then lower the oven temperature to 350°F/180°C and bake for an additional 50 minutes, or until the canelés are dark brown. Let the canelés cool in the molds for 5 minutes, then unmold them on a wire rack.

The canelés will keep for several days in a sealed container at room temperature.

2 cups plus
2 tablespoons /
500 ml whole milk

1 vanilla bean,
split lengthwise,
seeds scraped and
reserved

1 cup / 200 g
granulated sugar

1 cup / 120 g all-
purpose flour, sifted

3 large egg yolks, at
room temperature

2 tablespoons / 30 g
unsalted butter,
melted

¼ cup / 60 ml dark rum

NOTE: *Because I use silicone molds, I don't grease the molds. If you use metal molds, brush them well with melted butter.*

CANELÉS
DE BORDEAUX

BUGNES *with* ORANGE FLOWER WATER

When Mardi Gras season starts, every *boulangerie* in France sells *merveilles* and *bugnes*, heavenly little fritters that taste like old-fashioned charms. They are traditionally made in February and March because of the carnival festivities, but I like to make them at any time of year. It gives me great pleasure to see them puff up in the golden oil and then shower them with a generous amount of confectioners' sugar. My grandmother said they bring good luck and chase away bad spirits. Sounds like a good excuse to eat more of them.

PUT THE FLOUR in a large bowl and make a well in the center. Add the butter, eggs, granulated sugar, salt, baking powder, lemon and orange zests, and rum to the well. Mix everything together with your hands, gradually bringing the flour into the center. Shape into a ball, dust with flour, and wrap in plastic wrap. Refrigerate for 1 to 2 hours.

Dust a work surface with a little flour and roll out the dough ¼ inch/0.6 cm thick. With a pastry wheel or a knife, cut into 16-inch/40-cm-long bands that are 2 inches/5 cm wide. Then cut on the diagonal to make 5-inch/12.5-cm-long diamond shapes.

Heat 2 inches/5 cm of oil in a large pot over medium heat. Test the temperature of the oil (it should reach 320°F/160°C) by dropping in a small piece of dough—if it turns golden within seconds, the oil is ready for frying. Working in batches, add the dough to the oil and fry until golden and puffy, a few seconds or so on each side. Remove with a slotted spoon, drain on paper towels, and immediately sprinkle with confectioners' sugar. Serve hot.

SERVES 6

2 cups/240 g all-purpose flour, sifted, plus more for dusting

6 tablespoons/90 g unsalted butter, at room temperature

3 large eggs, at room temperature

½ cup/100 g granulated sugar

½ teaspoon fine sea salt

½ teaspoon baking powder

Grated zest of ½ lemon

Grated zest of ½ orange

2 tablespoons dark rum

Vegetable oil for deep-frying

Confectioners' sugar, sifted, for dusting

BLACK LOCUST
FLOWER FRITTERS

If scarcity makes things special, then this has to be one of the most special desserts there is. Black locust flowers are a favorite of honeybees, and only available a couple of precious weeks a year. Since the flowers lose their charm very fast, they really have to be fried almost immediately. I love having a big lunch in spring where everybody starts by gathering black locust flowers from the garden and then we eat them for dessert. They are so pretty on the plate, delicious, and, perhaps most important, so wonderful to imagine—is there anything more extraordinary than eating flowers?

IN A LARGE BOWL, whisk together the flour, granulated sugar, salt, eggs, milk, beer, vanilla, and rum, if using, to make a smooth batter. Cover and set aside to rest for 30 minutes to 1 hour.

Heat 1½ inches of oil in a medium pot over medium heat. To test if the oil is ready (it should reach 320°F/160°C), fry a few drops of batter; they should sizzle and turn golden brown within seconds. Working in small batches, dip the flowers in the batter, drain slightly, and fry until golden brown, 2 to 3 minutes per side. Remove the fritters with a slotted spoon and drain on paper towels. Dust lightly with confectioners' sugar and serve hot.

NOTE: *Make sure you use only black locust flowers, not yellow acacia flowers, which are toxic. If you feel the need to rinse the flowers, dry them well before frying. Only the flowers and little stems are edible, so be sure to throw out the rest!*

MAKES 20 TO 25
FRITTERS

2 cups/240 g all-
purpose flour

¼ cup/50 g granulated
sugar

½ teaspoon fine sea
salt

2 large eggs

¾ cup/200 ml whole
milk

⅔ cup/150 ml pale
lager or ale

1 teaspoon vanilla
extract

1 tablespoon dark rum
(optional)

Vegetable oil for
deep-frying

20 to 25 bunches of
unsprayed/organic
black locust flower
blossoms (see Note)

Confectioners' sugar
for dusting

SUGARED-ALMOND TART

Dragées are traditional sugar-coated almonds, given as small gifts at christenings and weddings, always tied in little silk pouches of white, pink, or blue. They are so pretty, and so sweet and crunchy, that when you start eating them, you just can't stop. This tart is a great excuse to have more dragées; there aren't enough weddings or christenings to satisfy my love for them. Because of the pastel colors of the almonds and their mini-egg shape, it's a tart I enjoy making for the kids at Easter time.

ON A LIGHTLY FLOURED surface, roll out the tart dough to a 12-inch/30-cm round about ¼ inch/0.5 mm thick. Transfer to a 10-inch/25-cm tart pan, press into the base and up the sides, and trim the edge. Prick the base with a fork. Cover with plastic wrap and freeze for 30 minutes.

Preheat the oven to 420°F/210°C.

Line the tart shell with parchment paper and fill with pie weights or dried beans. Bake until the sides begin to brown, about 15 minutes. Remove the tart from the oven and remove the paper and weights, then bake until the base starts to turn golden, about 5 minutes longer. Set aside to cool.

Combine the cream and the dragées in a medium saucepan, attach a candy thermometer to the side of the pan, and bring to a gentle boil. Cook until the mixture reduces by half, becomes thick and creamy, and reaches a temperature of 230°F/110°C. Remove from the heat and let cool completely.

Pour the cream into the tart and refrigerate for 4 to 5 hours before serving. The cream will set into a thick paste.

Sprinkle the reserved crushed dragées on top of the tart just before serving.

SERVES 6

Tart Dough (recipe follows)

1¼ cups/300 ml heavy cream

6 ounces/180 g dragées, coarsely crushed; reserve a handful for garnish

TART DOUGH

This short unsweetened dough, *pâte brisée*, works equally well for desserts (especially when the filling is on the sweeter side) and savory recipes. Double it to make enough for a double-crust pie.

IN A LARGE BOWL, mix the flour and salt. Add the butter and work it in with your fingers until the mixture is crumbly. Make a well in the center and add the egg and water. Mix until the dough comes together and forms a ball. Wrap in plastic wrap and refrigerate for at least 1 hour, or overnight.

MAKES ENOUGH
FOR ONE
10-INCH/25-CM
TART SHELL

- 2 cups/240 g all-purpose flour

- ½ teaspoon fine sea salt

- 9 tablespoons/ 125 g unsalted butter, cut into cubes and chilled

- 1 large egg

- 3 tablespoons cold water

SUMMER

Sometimes people play a game of conjuring up a fantasy meal where you invite anyone you'd like to a dinner party, from any period in history. I suppose I wouldn't mind a little soirée with some of my favorite celebrities. I would hold it in Paris at Le Grand Véfour, the most beautiful dining room in the world, where I was lucky enough to have my wedding lunch. Invitees would include Woody Allen and Sophia Loren and I would ask Alain Passard or Stephane Jégo to assist me in the kitchen (because I'd actually really want to cook at my own party—especially with those great chefs!). We'd have Champagne and foie gras and squab and a soufflé for dessert.

But my real fantasy meal, one I think about all the time, would take place in my garden at summer, with no one but our children and their families. By then, there would be lots of grandchildren and everyone would help me in the kitchen. We'd have an abundance of food on the table and many puppies under it, and at the end of the meal, I would look with pride over everything and think to myself, "You did it."

Of course, we have a small version of that meal every year—several of them, to be exact. In summer we are united, the seven children all with us for a lengthy period, and every day feels like a celebration. The day typically starts with a very late breakfast, anything from waffles or pancakes with fresh berries to a lovely omelet or *oeufs à la coque*. Then the cooking begins—if it wasn't already started the night before. By 2 or 3 o'clock in the afternoon, lunch is ready to be served. The children will gather from all corners of the house, some needing to be fished out of the pool, to help set the table. Because we are so many, we like to take one of our dining tables outside, and somehow this is always done at the last minute. I will be in the kitchen shouting, "It's ready, it's ready, it won't be good if it gets cold!" while chairs are rushed out of windows and doors; glasses, plates, and cutlery somehow make their way to the garden via a human conveyor belt formed by the kids. (Needless to say, I take the really fragile stuff out myself, just to be sure.) My husband tends to be suspiciously absent from these chaotic preparations, "tending to the dogs," he calls it.

Eating outside under the shade of a tree, with everybody who matters around me, is pure bliss. For the first few minutes, we hardly speak to each other, so busy are we eating. (It's fair to say we are a family of robust appetites.) My favorite moment is when I can finally relax, have that last sip of wine, and scoop up the remainder of the sauce with my bread. If I am lucky, and I often am, someone brings me coffee and my husband will tidy up in gentlemanly fashion, aided by some of the kids. That's when I head for the hammock. Before leaving the table, I usually say something like, "Let's make something light for dinner," and for a little while I really mean it. But an hour later, I often find myself back in the kitchen ready to do it all over again, just to re-create that magic moment.

In summer, I take one of the kids' wagons with me to the market. It is the season of plenty—every market stall bursting with peaches and apricots, plums and cherries—and I can't resist any of it. I buy crates of fruit, stacks of baguettes, too much of everything, I think. When I arrive home, I feel we are set for a week at least. But then the little mice sneak in and by the next day, there are only crumbs and perhaps a few odd vegetables that can be salvaged into a salad, and it's off to market again.

When I arrive at the fishmonger's on Saturday morning, I feel that every fish is calling to me, "Cook me, cook me!" As I align vegetables in a roasting pan for a tian or when I have just put several dozen freshly picked tomatoes on my table, I think there cannot be more beautiful colors anywhere. When I have fresh strawberries to serve with mascarpone cream, I am filled with delight. No matter how many trips I make to the market or how many feasts I plan, it always feels new and exciting to me.

I am someone who likes to exaggerate a bit. I have many "favorites" and quite a few things are "the best thing I have ever tasted." My husband often makes fun of me for this. But cooking for my family is my absolute favorite thing. Especially in summer.

STARTERS

Almond Gazpacho

Soupe au Pistou

Tomato Salad with Parsley and Shallots

Tomato Tart

Chilled Garden Pea Velouté

Tuna Rillettes

Spider Crab à la Basquaise

Almond Mussels

Vegetable Tian

MAIN COURSES AND A SIDE

Bouillabaisse

Langoustines with Armagnac

Mustard-Roasted Poussins

Duck Breasts Grilled over Grape Vines

Lyonnaise Sausage Roll

Calves' Liver à la Bordelaise

Black-Pig Pork Roast with Garlic Mashed Potatoes

My Couscous

DESSERTS

Peach and Cherry Papillotes

Red Berry Barquettes

Cherry Clafoutis

Strawberries in Wine with Mascarpone Cream

Coffee Cream Puffs

Hazelnut Blancmange

Pistachio Sabayon with Strawberries and Meringues

Apricot Panna Cotta

Chilled White Peaches in White Wine Syrup

ALMOND GAZPACHO

Although this chilled soup has a creamy texture, it is surprisingly refreshing. It's a recipe I make sparingly, though: it has an unusual (in a good way) and somewhat fancy (for lack of a better word) flavor, and it reminds me of the soups you get in modern restaurants in Spain, the sort of places that have tasting menus with a different wine for every course. If I'm planning a very special dinner for guests, I might first serve foie gras on toast, then a small bowl of this soup, then fish, then meat, and then cheese, dessert, and canelés (see page 69), just because we are in Bordeaux. You get the picture.

SOAK THE BREAD in a bowl of cool water for 1 minute, then drain, squeezing out as much water as possible.

Transfer the bread to a food processor and add the almonds, grapes, cucumber, and minced garlic. Start processing and gradually add the ice water, ⅔ cup/150 ml of the olive oil, the vinegar, and salt and pepper to taste. Purée until you have a smooth and velvety mixture.

Pass the soup though a fine sieve into a bowl. Cover and refrigerate for at least 3 hours, or overnight.

Just before serving, heat the remaining 2 teaspoons olive oil in a small sauté pan over medium heat and cook the sliced garlic until golden and crispy, about 3 minutes. Add the reserved almonds and toast for a minute or two.

Ladle the chilled gazpacho into individual bowls. Sprinkle with the fried garlic and almonds, and piment d'Espelette, add a drizzle of olive oil, and serve immediately.

SERVES 4

- 2 cups/150 g cubed crustless white bread
- 1⅓ cups/200 g slivered blanched almonds (reserve 2 tablespoons for garnish)
- 1⅔ cups/250 g seedless green grapes
- 1 medium cucumber, peeled, halved lengthwise, and seeded
- 2 garlic cloves, minced, plus 2 garlic cloves, sliced
- 3 cups/700 ml ice-cold water
- ⅔ cup/150 ml plus 2 teaspoons extra-virgin olive oil, plus more for drizzling
- 2 tablespoons sherry vinegar
- Fine sea salt and freshly ground black pepper
- ¼ teaspoon piment d'Espelette

SOUPE AU PISTOU

To me, this Provençal soup is very much the French version of a minestrone, and while I would not go so far to say that it's an improvement on the original, it's at least a very nice alternative. The people of Provence did a two-for-one deal, also borrowing a pesto recipe from their Italian neighbors to mix into the soup, which makes for a very rare Franco-Italian invention. Provençal pesto is usually made without pine nuts and some versions add tomatoes to the mix, which I like. Leftover pistou is lovely on grilled bread with aperitifs. So many of the soups I make are thick and velvety, so when a change is called for, it's great to have in my repertoire a tasty clear one studded with goodies.

START THE SOUP a day ahead: Rinse the dried beans and soak them in cold water overnight.

Drain the beans and put them in a large saucepan. Add the bay leaf and enough water to cover the beans by 3 inches/7.5 cm, bring to a simmer, and simmer until the beans are tender, about 1½ hours. Drain and set aside.

In a large pot, heat the olive oil over medium heat. Add the haricots verts, tomatoes, zucchini, onions, carrots, leek, and garlic and sauté for 4 minutes. Add the water and thyme and season with salt and pepper. Bring to a boil, cover, lower the heat, and simmer for 10 minutes.

Add the macaroni and cook until al dente, 8 to 10 minutes.

While the pasta is cooking, make the pistou. Combine the basil and garlic in a mortar and pound to a paste. Gradually add olive oil, Parmesan, and coarse salt and pepper to taste. Stir in the tomato.

For the soup

8 ounces/250 g dried white beans

8 ounces/250 g dried kidney beans

1 bay leaf

2 tablespoons extra-virgin olive oil

8 ounces/250 g haricots verts, cut into ¼-inch/1-cm-thick slices

4 tomatoes, peeled, halved, seeded, and diced

3 zucchini, diced

3 onions, thinly sliced

2 carrots, peeled and diced

1 leek, white and pale green parts, thinly sliced

5 garlic cloves, thinly sliced

6 cups/1.5 l water

A few sprigs of fresh thyme

Fine sea salt and freshly ground black pepper

1 cup/140 g small elbow macaroni

For the pistou

2 bunches fresh basil, leaves removed and chopped

5 garlic cloves

5 tablespoons/75 ml extra-virgin olive oil

⅔ cup/60 g freshly grated Parmesan cheese, plus more for sprinkling

Coarse sea salt and freshly ground black pepper

1 ripe tomato, peeled, halved, seeded, and diced

Add the cooked beans to the soup. Season with fine salt and pepper.

Ladle the soup into bowls and add a spoon of pistou to each. Sprinkle with Parmesan cheese and serve immediately.

TOMATO SALAD *with* PARSLEY *and* SHALLOTS

In the height of summer, we will almost certainly have one out of two salads every day: the Italian Caprese, which is now served in practically every French restaurant as "tomate-mozza," or this "French" tomato salad with raw shallots. The rule of thumb goes something like this: If we have pasta for lunch, we will most likely pair it with the Italian version. If we have fish or cold cuts, we go for the French salad. This is a very simple recipe, of course, but one I thought I had to include because it's such a big part of what we enjoy at our daily table.

WHISK TOGETHER the shallots, mustard, and olive oil in a small bowl and season with salt and pepper.

Arrange the tomatoes on a serving plate. Drizzle the shallot vinaigrette over the tomatoes and scatter the parsley on top.

SERVES 4

3 shallots, minced

1 teaspoon Dijon mustard

½ cup / 120 ml extra-virgin olive oil

Fine sea salt and freshly ground pepper

5 or 6 ripe heirloom tomatoes, sliced ½ inch thick

A bunch of fresh parsley, leaves removed and finely chopped

SHALLOTS

It seems that the Bordelaise can't live without shallots, or wine, and both are high on my list of favorites. You will find shallots in recipes all over this book, cooked, reduced with sauces, sliced and served raw on top of meat. If I gave cooking lessons, the first thing I would say is, "A shallot is not an onion."

TOMATO TART

There are the tomatoes readily available in supermarkets, which are often hard, watery, and fairly flavorless. And then there are the locally grown tomatoes of summer, which come in a variety of shapes and sizes, shades and colors, ranging from dark greens and yellows to deep orange reds. They have intriguing names and many of them taste so good that they explain in a single bite why the tomato is really a fruit, not a vegetable. Over the last few years, these tomatoes have spoiled my palate for any other kind. I have them on their own, with just a little olive oil, or in salads or in tarts, which really bring out their flavor. I make many different kinds of tomato tarts, but I think this is the one I like best.

Tart Dough
(page 79)

All-purpose flour
for rolling

A few sprigs of
fresh basil, leaves
removed and
chopped, plus more
whole leaves for
serving

1 tablespoon grainy
mustard

¼ cup/60 ml extra-
virgin olive oil

Fine sea salt and
freshly ground black
pepper

2 tablespoons tomato
paste

1¼ pounds/550 g
tomatoes, sliced
¼ inch thick

1 tablespoon honey

1 small ball buffalo
mozzarella (about
5 ounces/125 g),
torn into small
pieces

ON A LIGHTLY FLOURED surface, roll out the dough to a 12 inch/30 cm round about ¼ inch/0.5 mm thick. Press into the base and sides of a 10-inch/25-cm tart pan and trim the edges. Prick the base with a fork. Put the pan in the refrigerator to chill for 30 minutes.

Preheat the oven to 350°F/180°C.

Combine the basil, mustard, 2 tablespoons of the olive oil, and a pinch of salt in a blender. Puree until smooth.

Spread the tomato paste over the base of the tart shell and then pour the basil oil over it. Arrange the sliced tomatoes in a circular pattern, in one layer, in the tart shell. Season with salt and pepper. Drizzle the honey and the remaining 2 tablespoons olive oil over the tomatoes.

Bake until the pastry is golden, about 35 minutes. Let the tart rest for 15 minutes.

Scatter the mozzarella and some basil over the tart before serving.

CHILLED GARDEN
PEA VELOUTÉ

On warm summer days, it feels so luxurious to have a chilled vegetable soup. I probably make gazpacho most often—every other day, in fact—but this pea soup is a beautiful alternative. If I have stale bread, I like to quickly make croûtons (see page 107) with some olive oil and rosemary, but most often I just serve it with a fresh baguette. As is the case with gazpacho, I think it makes a world of difference to have just a hint of garlic cream and oil sprinkled over the soup.

HEAT 1 TABLESPOON of the butter in a large pot over medium heat. Add the peas, potatoes, onion, and sliced garlic and cook for 4 minutes. Add the stock, season with salt and pepper, and bring to a boil, then reduce the heat and simmer until vegetables are tender, about 20 minutes.

Working in batches, purée the soup in a blender until smooth. Pour the soup into a large bowl and allow to cool, then cover and chill in the refrigerator for at least 1 hour.

In a small bowl, combine the minced garlic and the cream and whisk together for 10 seconds. Set aside for 10 minutes.

Cook the bacon in a large sauté pan over medium heat until golden and crisp, about 3 minutes per side. Drain on paper towels.

Just before serving the soup, pass the garlic cream through a sieve, pressing on the garlic; discard the garlic.

Serve the soup drizzled with the garlic cream and a dash of olive oil and topped with the bacon slices.

SERVES 6

3 tablespoons unsalted butter

1⅓ pounds / 600 g peas in the pod, shelled

2 medium russet potatoes, peeled and diced

1 onion, sliced

2 garlic cloves, thinly sliced, plus 1 garlic clove, minced

6 cups / 1.5 liters chicken or vegetable stock

Fine sea salt and freshly ground black pepper

½ cup / 120 ml heavy cream

6 slices good-quality bacon

Extra-virgin olive oil for drizzling

TUNA RILLETTES

Rillettes are pâté-like spreads that usually consist of chunky bits of meat that have been cooked in their own fat. You find them everywhere in France; many families have their own recipes and most butchers offer more than one variety. The most common version is made of pork, but there are no rules, and I've had more types than I can remember. I am particularly fond of tuna rillettes, which are less fatty than those made from meat and are a great starter or amuse-bouche served on toast. The texture and flavor is at once fishy and creamy, somewhere between a tuna tartare and a terrine. I suppose you will just have to try this.

IN A MEDIUM SAUCEPAN, steam the fish on a rack over boiling water until it is just cooked through, 6 to 8 minutes. Let cool for 15 minutes.

Using a fork, flake the tuna into a bowl. Add the olive oil, crème fraîche, lemon juice, shallot, parsley, chives, pink pepper, and salt and black pepper to taste. Cover and chill in the refrigerator for at least 3 hours, or overnight.

Serve the rillettes on grilled baguette slices.

SERVES 4

12 ounces / 350 g tuna belly

¼ cup / 60 ml extra-virgin olive oil

⅓ cup / 80 ml crème fraîche or sour cream

1 tablespoon fresh lemon juice

1 shallot, minced

2 tablespoons finely chopped fresh parsley

2 tablespoons finely chopped fresh chives

¼ teaspoon pink peppercorns, finely ground

Fine sea salt and freshly ground black pepper

Grilled slices of baguette or country bread

SPIDER CRAB À LA BASQUAISE

Crab is very high on my list of favorite foods, maybe in the top three. Anything from hairy crab to soft-shell crab to spider crab—if it's on the menu, I will order it, especially this particular wonderfully spicy, aromatic dish. Usually I refrain from any sort of gimmicks when serving a dish; I like a good honest *cocotte* on the table, and more often than not I place the less-than-pretty roasting pan in front of my guests. So, while I still love '80s music, when I think of some of the overwrought dishes I had in those days, complete with raspberry coulis, I have to shudder. In this case, however, putting the meat back into the shells feels authentic and traditional rather than show-offy.

Cooking any kind of crab usually requires a lot of work; this recipe is no exception, but I think it merits the care.

COOK THE CRABS. Plunge them in a large pot of cold water seasoned with the coarse salt and peppercorns. Add the bay leaf and thyme and bring to a boil over medium-high heat, then cover, reduce the heat to medium, and gently boil the crabs for 15 minutes. Drain the crabs and let cool for 15 minutes.

Preheat the broiler.

Meanwhile, trying to keep the top shells mostly intact, pick all the meat from the spider crabs with the help of a crab pick, a small teaspoon, and a claw cracker. Rinse the top shells and reserve.

Heat the olive oil in a large sauté pan over medium heat. Add the onion, leek, fennel, garlic, and shallot and cook until golden, about 6 minutes. Add the tomato and season with the fine salt and ground black pepper. Add the saffron, piment d'Espelette, and crabmeat, stir, and cook for 25 seconds,

SERVES 2

2 spider or snow crabs
  (4 pounds / 2 kg total)

3 tablespoons coarse
  sea salt

1 teaspoon black
  peppercorns

1 bay leaf

2 sprigs of fresh thyme

2 tablespoons extra-
  virgin olive oil

1 small onion, finely
  chopped

½ leek, white part
  only, finely chopped

½ fennel bulb, finely
  chopped

2 garlic cloves, minced

1 shallot, minced

½ cup / 75 g diced
  tomato

  Fine sea salt and
  freshly ground black
  pepper

¼ teaspoon saffron
  threads

  A dash of piment
  d'Espelette

¼ cup / 60 ml dry white
  wine

2 teaspoons fresh
  lemon juice

½ cup / 30 g fresh
  bread crumbs

2 tablespoons chopped
  fresh parsley

2 tablespoons unsalted
  butter

letting the spices release their aroma. Pour in the white wine and simmer over medium heat to reduce slightly, 2 to 3 minutes. Stir in the lemon juice.

Scoop the crab mixture into the shells, sprinkle with the bread crumbs and parsley, and dot with the butter. Put the crab on a baking sheet and broil until golden and bubbly, about 5 minutes. Serve hot.

ALMOND MUSSELS

When I am shopping for mussels, somehow a line from Oscar Wilde's *The Importance of Being Earnest* always pops into my head, reminding me to get them when they look pretty and to skip them when they don't. (The quote is much more apt when applied to mussels than women, in my mind.) That leaves how to prepare them. *Moules marinière* is as classic as any dish in France (or Belgium), lovely with French fries. When I am in Normandy, having them with cream is a must. At home, I seem to make them most often with sausage meat or, as in this case, with almonds. This version makes a nice starter; I place a big baking dish of them on the table outside and guests can nibble on the mussels while sipping crisp white wine and awaiting the next course.

SERVES 4 TO 6

1 cup / 60 g fresh bread crumbs

7 tablespoons / 80 g unsalted butter, at room temperature

A bunch of fresh parsley, leaves removed and finely chopped

3 garlic cloves, minced

Fine sea salt and freshly ground black pepper

1½ cups / 180 g finely ground almonds

4 pounds / 2 kg mussels, scrubbed if necessary

COMBINE THE BREAD CRUMBS, butter, parsley, and garlic in a bowl, season with salt and pepper, and mix well. Mix in the almonds. The mixture will have the consistency of a paste.

Preheat the oven to 425°F / 220°C.

Put the mussels in a large pot, cover, and cook over high heat until they just open, a few minutes. Remove from the heat, uncover, and let cool slightly.

Discard any mussels that did not open. Remove one half shell from each mussel, and arrange them mussel-side up in a shallow baking dish. Scoop about ½ teaspoon of the stuffing onto each mussel. Season with salt and pepper.

Transfer the baking dish to the oven and bake until the surface of the mussels is golden and bubbly, about 6 minutes. Serve immediately.

VEGETABLE TIAN

This is a simply gorgeous ratatouille-like dish that is equally good served on its own or as a side dish with fish or meat. It's so beautiful I always think it must have served as an inspiration for the ratatouille in the Pixar film of the same name. It's a reminder that the outcome depends not only on the ingredients we put into a dish but also how we use them. I love a classic, mushy ratatouille with a fried egg on top and a slightly crunchy ratatouille (see page 187) for serving with slow-cooked lamb. But I make this stunning tian when I care as much about how the dish looks as I do how it tastes.

PREHEAT THE OVEN to 400°F/200°C.

Slice the tomatoes, zucchini, and eggplant into thin rounds, no thicker than ⅛ inch/3 mm. You can use a mandoline if you have one.

Put the eggplant in a colander set in the sink, sprinkle with the coarse salt, and let sit for 20 minutes. This will help extract some of the bitterness from the eggplant.

Bring 2 cups/475 ml water to a boil. Pour over the eggplant to rinse and let drain, then gently pat dry with a paper towel.

Rub the halved garlic clove all over an 8 × 12-inch/20 × 30-cm baking dish. Starting from the outside and working your way in, arrange the sliced vegetables, alternating them in tight rows. Sprinkle the sliced garlic, the thyme, and bay leaves on top, drizzle with the olive oil, and season with salt and pepper.

Bake until the vegetables are just tender, about 30 minutes. Sprinkle with the parsley and serve immediately.

SERVES 6

4 large tomatoes

3 large zucchini

2 medium eggplant

1½ tablespoons coarse sea salt

2 garlic cloves, thinly sliced, plus 1 garlic clove, halved

8 sprigs of fresh thyme

3 bay leaves

3 tablespoons extra-virgin olive oil for drizzling

Fine sea salt and freshly ground black pepper

A handful of finely chopped fresh parsley

LANGOUSTINES *with* ARMAGNAC

Comfort dishes are usually associated with the colder months, but this is my summery comfort dish. I would love to come home from the beach, feeling slightly chilly, on a day when the clouds have gathered, and find it waiting for me. In reality, I would probably make it myself for everyone—but you can always hope. I know I have a habit of mentioning dipping bread into sauces, and while it's always enjoyable, here it would simply be a crime not to scoop up all the wonderful juices.

SERVES 4

24 fresh langoustines (alternatively you can use jumbo shrimp, preferably head-on)

6 tablespoons/90 ml extra-virgin olive oil

Fine sea salt and freshly ground black pepper

6 shallots, minced

3 sprigs of fresh thyme, leaves only

1 cup/240 ml dry white wine

2 tablespoons/30 ml Armagnac

PREHEAT THE OVEN to 400°F/210°C.

Put each langoustine belly-side down on a cutting board and cut lengthwise in half, from head to tail. Reserve the juices in a small bowl.

In a large sauté pan, heat 3 tablespoons of the olive oil over high heat until nearly smoking. Add the langoustines, season with salt and pepper, and cook briskly until the flesh becomes opaque, about 4 minutes. Transfer the langoustines to a baking dish.

Add the remaining 3 tablespoons olive oil to the sauté pan and heat over medium heat. Cook the shallots until translucent and slightly tender, about 4 minutes. Sprinkle with the thyme leaves, add the white wine, and simmer to reduce for 2 to 3 minutes. Pour over the langoustines.

Bake the langoustines until lightly golden, about 10 minutes.

Heat the Armagnac in a saucepan over very low heat. Remove the langoustines from the oven and pour the warm Armagnac over them. Quickly light a match, and carefully ignite the liquid to flambé the langoustines. Serve immediately.

MUSTARD-ROASTED POUSSINS

I find it very satisfying to have a whole bird in front of me, all to myself. While I like quail and squab, they are not quite the same as chicken, and you need two to feel satisfied. *Coquelets*, also known as poussins or spring chickens, offer a perfect solution. With all the qualities of a chicken but small in size, they are the ultimate answer to the whole "do you want breast or leg?" problem. Instead of serving mustard on the side as one might do with a whole roast chicken, I like rub a mustard–wine fraîche mixture all over the birds, inside and out too. Tucking halved new potatoes (but of course) underneath and around the poussins as they roast makes for a delicious built-in side dish.

IN A SMALL BOWL, mix the mustard, crème fraîche, butter, lemon juice, garlic, and nutmeg until smooth.

Rinse the chickens and pat dry. Rub the chickens inside and out with the mustard mixture. Season with salt and pepper. Cover and refrigerate for at least 2 hours, or overnight.

Preheat the oven to 350°F/180°C.

Put the potatoes in a saucepan, cover with cold salted water, and bring to a boil, then reduce the heat and simmer for 10 minutes; the potatoes will only be partially cooked. Drain.

Put the poussins in individual baking dishes or a large roasting pan. Scatter the potatoes around them, drizzle everything with olive oil, and season with salt and pepper. Roast until the poussins are golden and cooked through (the juices should run clear, not pink, when you prick the thigh with a knife), about 40 minutes. Cover with foil if the birds are getting too dark.

Serve 1 poussin per person, accompanied by the potatoes.

SERVES 4

½ cup/120 g Dijon mustard

¼ cup/60 ml crème fraîche

4 tablespoons/60 g unsalted butter, at room temperature

Juice of ½ lemon

2 garlic cloves, minced

¼ teaspoon grated nutmeg

Four 1½-pound/ 680-g poussins or guinea hens

Fine sea salt and freshly ground black pepper

Extra-virgin olive oil for drizzling

2 pounds/900 g small new potatoes (about 20), peeled and halved

DUCK BREASTS GRILLED OVER GRAPEVINES

Duck breasts, or *magrets de canard*, are very much a usual suspect in traditional French bistros. I have countless memories of sitting with my parents in such establishments, eating duck breasts with rich sauces and sautéed potatoes. But now that I'm older, I feel that duck (perhaps my favorite meat) doesn't really need creamy sauces, and so I like to pan-sear it and serve it with peaches sautéed in the duck fat, a dreamy combination. To add an extra touch to the dish, I sometimes grill the duck breasts for the final minutes over grapevines so they get a bit smoky and infused with the taste of the vines. So Médoc!

PUT THE DUCK BREASTS fat-side up on a large plate. With a sharp knife, score the fat in a crisscross pattern. Season the duck on both sides with coarse salt and pepper, making sure to rub the salt inside the cuts. (This will add an extra tasty and crunchy touch to the meat when you cook it.)

Put some dried grapevines in a grill and light a fire.

Put the breasts in a large sauté pan (cook in two batches if your pan will not hold all of them comfortably), turn the heat on to medium-low, and start precooking the duck breasts. As they cook, the duck fat will render and you will need to periodically pour the fat off into a bowl. Cook for 5 minutes, skin-side down, then flip the breasts over and cook for 1 minute. Transfer to a plate. Reserve the duck fat.

When the branches have ashed over, transfer the duck breasts to the grill and cook, uncovered, until medium-rare, 5 to 7 minutes on each side. Let the duck breasts rest on a cutting board for 5 minutes.

SERVES 6

4 large duck breasts (magrets de canard), about 12 ounces / 350 g each

Coarse sea salt and freshly ground black pepper

A large bunch of dried grapevines (*sarments de vignes*)

8 yellow peaches, peeled, pitted, and quartered

4 shallots, minced

While the duck is resting, heat 2 tablespoons of the reserved duck fat in a large sauté pan over medium heat. Cook the peaches until golden on both of the cut sides, about 6 minutes.

Slice the duck breasts into ½-inch/1-cm-thick slices. Sprinkle the minced shallots over duck breasts and serve with the peaches.

LYONNAISE SAUSAGE ROLL

This is essentially meat in bread. I *adore* meat in bread. I spent my graduate school days in England munching away on everything from Cornish pasties and kidney pies to beef Wellington. Bringing this obsession back to France, I became a keen admirer of *pâté en croûte* and fell in love with the Lyonnaise sausage roll. I appreciate a good brioche, and when you put a good sausage into it (like a *cervelas de Lyon*), it only improves it.

PUT THE FLOUR IN A BOWL. Make a well in the center and add the yeast and 1 tablespoon warm water. Let the yeast proof for 2 to 3 minutes. Add the sugar, 3 of the eggs, and the butter and knead for 8 to 10 minutes, until you get a soft and elastic dough that's slightly on the sticky side. Shape into a ball.

Grease a large bowl with butter and add the dough. Cover the dough with a damp cloth and let rise in a warm environment until doubled in size, about 2 hours.

Meanwhile, put the sausages in a saucepan of cold water and bring to a boil over medium heat. Reduce the heat and simmer until cooked through, up to 25 minutes, depending upon the type of sausage. Drain and let cool, then peel off the sausage casings.

Preheat the oven 400°F/200°C. Butter a 9 × 4-inch/24 × 9-cm loaf pan.

On a lightly floured surface, roll the dough into a 10-inch/25-cm-long rectangle about 7 inches/18 cm wide and about ½ inch/1 cm thick. Lightly whisk the remaining egg to make an egg wash.

2 cups/240 g all-purpose flour, sifted, plus more for rolling

2 teaspoons/10 g active dry yeast

1 tablespoon warm water

1½ tablespoons granulated sugar

4 large eggs

7 tablespoons/100 g unsalted butter, at room temperature, plus more for the bowl and pan

1 large good-quality pork sausage, 8 inches/20 cm long and a scant 2 inches/4.5 cm thick

Arrange the sausages in a line down the center of the dough and fold it over to encase the sausages. Fold over the ends to seal the roll. Put the sausage roll seam-side down in the pan, and brush with the egg wash.

Bake until well risen and golden brown, about 25 minutes. Let cool on a wire rack for at least 10 minutes before serving warm, sliced 1½ inches / 4cm thick.

CALVES' LIVER À LA BORDELAISE

A calves' liver is a staple at any decent bistro, and while it's not my very favorite dish, I always like to see it on a menu. I think to myself, *If I find nothing else, I can always order the liver*. Here in Médoc they add shallots to most dishes and wine to everything, including liver. While there are several versions of *foie de veau à la Bordelaise*, I prefer this one with white wine and Bayonne ham. It should go without saying that care should be taken not to overcook the liver, or it will become dry.

PUT THE CALVES' LIVER on a large plate. Season with salt and pepper and dust lightly on both sides with flour.

In a large sauté pan, heat 2 tablespoons of the butter with the olive oil over medium heat. Cook the liver until browned on both sides and medium-rare to medium inside, 4 to 5 minutes per side. (Add a few more minutes if you prefer your liver well done.) Transfer to a plate and keep warm.

Wipe out the sauté pan and add 2 tablespoons of the butter. Cook the shallots and garlic over medium heat until lightly golden, about 5 minutes. Add the white wine and simmer to reduce by half, 3 to 4 minutes. Remove from the heat, swirl in 1 tablespoon of the butter, and season with salt and pepper. The sauce should be glossy and not too thick.

Meanwhile, heat a small sauté pan over medium heat and add the remaining tablespoon of butter. Cook the ham for a few seconds on each side, until golden and slightly crisp.

Serve the slices of liver draped with the slices of ham and drizzled with the shallot-wine sauce.

SERVES 4

Four 4- to 5-ounce / 110- to 125-g slices calves' liver

Fine sea salt and freshly ground black pepper

All-purpose flour for dusting

6 tablespoons / 90g unsalted butter

1 tablespoon extra-virgin olive oil

4 shallots, minced

2 garlic cloves, minced

½ cup / 120 ml dry white wine

4 thin slices Bayonne ham or prosciutto

BLACK-PIG PORK ROAST *with* GARLIC MASHED POTATOES

The Noir de Bigorre is an ancient breed of pig, dating back to prehistoric times. Native to the mountains between France and Spain, the Pyrenees, it just may be the tastiest pig on earth. One fine summer day, when I was having guests for dinner and really wanted to spoil them, I bought a big piece of Noir de Bigorre pork loin and asked my trusted butcher, M. Manenti, to wrap the meat in finely sliced pork belly from the same breed. He advised me not to preheat the oven and to slow-cook the pork roast at a low temperature so the meat would cook gently in the melting fat. If you want melt-in-your-mouth succulent meat, this is it. Seek out the best-quality pork you can find for this recipe. I serve this dish with an apple compote and extra-rich garlic mashed potatoes.

SEASON THE PORK LOIN all over with coarse salt and pepper. Put the pork in a roasting pan and scatter the garlic cloves and thyme around it. Drizzle everything with the olive oil.

Transfer the roasting pan to the oven and turn the heat on to 275°F/140°C. Roast the pork until it reaches an internal temperature of 145°F/63°C, about 1 hour and 15 minutes. To test if the meat is cooked if you don't have a meat thermometer, insert a skewer in the thickest part—juices that run out should be clear, with no trace of pinkness. Let rest on a cutting board for 15 minutes.

Slice the roast into ½-inch/1.5-cm-thick slices and serve with the mashed potatoes and roasted garlic cloves.

(recipe continues)

SERVES 6

One 3-pound/ 1.3-kg pork loin roast, wrapped in 6 to 8 thin slices of pork belly or bacon

Coarse sea salt and freshly ground black pepper

20 garlic cloves, unpeeled

A few sprigs of fresh thyme

¼ cup/60 ml extra-virgin olive oil for drizzling

Garlic Mashed Potatoes (recipe follows)

GARLIC MASHED POTATOES

Potatoes should not be taken lightly. To begin with, they are my mother-in-law's favorite food. They have an important job as well: to soak up the sauce of a good roast or braise. A hint of garlic, a touch of cream—these are the touches that elevate mashed potatoes to stars in their own right.

PUT THE POTATOES in a pot, cover with cold salted water, and bring to a full boil over medium heat. Season with salt and cook until potatoes are tender, 10 to 15 minutes.

Drain the potatoes well, return to the pot, and mash with a potato masher. Add the cream, butter, and garlic and mix with a wooden spoon until smooth. Reheat over low heat if necessary. Season with salt and pepper. Serve immediately, or keep warm in a double boiler for up to 1 hour.

SERVES 6

2 pounds / 900 g new
  potatoes, peeled and
  sliced ½ inch / 1.5 cm
  thick

Fine sea salt

¼ cup / 60 ml heavy
  cream

4 tablespoons / 60 g
  unsalted butter, at
  room temperature

2 garlic cloves, minced

Freshly ground
  black pepper

GARLIC

I don't think a day goes by when I don't cook with garlic. It's always there in my kitchen, ready to be crushed, baked, roasted, sliced, caramelized, or rubbed on bread. In winter, I love to break open a stubborn head of dry garlic and watch the papery white flakes and copper-colored cloves arrange themselves on my kitchen table. In spring, I marvel at the rich color of fresh purple garlic, and I enjoy cooking every bit of it, including the stalks. The symbol of this country is a proud rooster. A funny moustache, a bottle of wine, a baguette, and a piece of cheese are the most celebrated icons. But let's face it: garlic is a big thing in French cooking.

PEACH *and* CHERRY PAPILLOTES

Many good things in the world of gastronomy have had strange or unexpected routes to our tables. Some came from the need to preserve food or from lack of alternatives, or were happened upon by chance—as was the case with Champagne. This simple yet luscious dish was born out of two things: my having too much fruit and having too little time to do anything complicated with it. So the fruit ended up in a parchment envelope, a technique I most often use to cook fish. The result was satisfying, to say the least, and so this has become my go-to summer dessert when I have no time to make dessert.

PREHEAT THE OVEN to 400°F/200°C.

In a small saucepan, combine ⅓ cup/65 g of the sugar and the wine and bring to a low boil, stirring to dissolve the sugar. Lower the heat slightly and cook, stirring occasionally, until the mixture thickens to a syrup, 5 to 6 minutes. Set aside to cool.

Cut a 12 × 18-inch/30 cm × 46-cm rectangle of parchment paper or aluminum foil. Add the fruit to one side of the paper, along with the vanilla seeds and bean. Sprinkle the verbena leaves on top and drizzle with the red wine syrup. Sprinkle with the remaining tablespoon of sugar. Fold the paper over the fruit and seal the papillote by folding the edges tightly together over themselves all around.

Put the papillote on a rimmed baking sheet and bake for 10 minutes, or until the fruit is slightly cooked.

Carefully open the package and spoon the fruit and sauce onto plates, discarding the verbena and vanilla bean. Serve warm.

SERVES 4

⅓ cup/65 g granulated
   sugar, plus
   1 tablespoon for
   sprinkling

⅓ cup/80 ml dry red
   wine

4 yellow peaches,
   pitted and sliced

25 cherries, stemmed,
   halved, and pitted

1 vanilla bean,
   cut in half, split
   lengthwise, seeds
   scraped out, seeds
   and bean reserved

   A handful of fresh
   verbena or mint
   leaves

RED BERRY BARQUETTES

I have an obsession with barquette molds because they look like old-fashioned baskets—and what better to fill them with than freshly picked berries? My children love making this recipe, as it's simple but very rewarding. If you don't have barquette molds, you can use any individual-sized tartlet molds.

———————————— ✺ ————————————

MAKE THE DOUGH. Sift the flour into a large bowl and make a well in the center. Add the sugar, salt, egg yolks, and butter to the well and gradually mix the ingredients with your hands until you have a soft, elastic dough. Shape into a ball, wrap in plastic wrap, and refrigerate for at least 1 hour, or overnight.

On a lightly floured work surface, roll the dough out ¼ inch/0.5 cm thick. Cut into ovals and then line 8 barquette molds (4 to 5 inches/10 to 12 cm long) with the dough. Put in the freezer for 30 minutes.

Preheat the oven to 400°F/200°C.

Line the barquettes with parchment paper and fill with pie weights or dried beans. Bake the tartlet shells until golden, about 10 minutes. Remove from the oven and set aside to cool. Remove the parchment paper and weights.

Heat the cranberry jelly with the water in a small saucepan over medium-low heat, stirring occasionally, until melted and smooth, a minute or two. Remove from the heat.

With a pastry brush, brush the bases of the barquette shells with the cranberry glaze. Fill with the berries and brush again with the cranberry glaze. These tartlets are best eaten the same day.

SERVES 8

For the dough

1½ cups/180 g all-purpose flour, plus more for rolling

⅓ cup/65 g granulated sugar

A pinch of fine sea salt

3 large egg yolks

7 tablespoons/100 g unsalted butter, cut into cubes, at room temperature

For the filling

5 tablespoons cranberry jelly

1 tablespoon water

1 pound/450 g fresh berries, such as red currants, strawberries, raspberries—any red summer berries will do

CHERRY CLAFOUTIS

I adore the period in early summer when you can still get beautiful peonies at the market and cherries and apricots have started showing up in the stalls. The grass is still green and vivid, before the scorching temperatures of July and August take away its luster; there are no crowds at the beach; and the summer has still so much promise and winter seems an eternity away. I must admit that I don't really use cherries much for cooking, though we buy bags and bags. It seems that no sooner have I put them in a bowl on our kitchen table, often mixed with apricots, than little hands have grabbed them all. Occasionally there are enough to have them with ice cream, or to make this cherry clafoutis, a family favorite. I leave the pits in, as I find they add to the flavor and somehow make the clafoutis more authentic—rustic and appealing. Just be sure to warn your guests about the pits!

3½ tablespoons unsalted butter, melted, plus more for the cake pan

1 pound / 450 g cherries, stemmed

Scant ¾ cup / 70 g all-purpose flour

⅓ cup / 65 g granulated sugar

Pinch of fine sea salt

1 vanilla bean, split lengthwise, seeds scraped out and reserved

¾ cup plus 1½ tablespoons / 200 ml whole milk

4 large eggs

1 tablespoon orange flower water

Confectioners' sugar for dusting

PREHEAT THE OVEN to 400°F / 200°C.

Generously butter a 9-inch / 23-cm round cake pan. Arrange the cherries in the bottom of the cake pan.

In a large bowl, whisk together the flour, granulated sugar, salt, and vanilla seeds. Whisking gently, add the milk and then the eggs, one by one. Add the orange flower water and melted butter and mix until you get a smooth batter. Pour the batter over the cherries.

Bake for 15 minutes. Lower the oven temperature to 350°F / 180°C and bake until the clafoutis has puffed up and lightly browned, about an additional 30 minutes. Let cool on a rack and set for at least 1 hour.

Just before serving, sprinkle with confectioners' sugar.

STRAWBERRIES IN WINE
with MASCARPONE CREAM

Fresh strawberries and red Bordeaux may seem like unlikely allies, but some-how they go perfectly together. I like to make a little cocktail with red wine and strawberries, and one day I thought of pairing them in a dessert instead. Truthfully, this is really just an upgraded version of the unbeatable combi-nation of strawberries and whipped cream, but adding wine and mascarpone gives the traditional duo zing and a touch of grown-up decadence.

PUT THE STRAWBERRIES in a large bowl and pour the wine over them. Sprinkle in the granulated sugar and stir to combine. Cover and refrigerate for at least 4 hours, or up 12 hours.

Just before serving, in a medium bowl, whisk together the cream, mascar-pone, vanilla seeds, and confectioners' sugar to taste until stiff peaks form.

Spoon a generous amount of the whipped cream into each dessert bowl or ramekin. Top with the strawberries and wine sauce.

SERVES 6

¾ to 1 pound / 350 g to 450 g strawberries, hulled and halved or quartered, depending on size

1 cup / 250 ml dry red wine, preferably a Bordeaux

¼ cup / 50 g granulated sugar

¾ cup / 180 ml heavy cream

½ cup / 120 ml mascarpone

2 vanilla beans, split lengthwise, seeds scraped out and reserved

2 to 3 tablespoons confectioners' sugar, sifted

COFFEE CREAM PUFFS

I am not a big snacker. Sometimes I'll have a few chips or chocolates but I am pretty faithful to regular meal hours—and teatime, of course. But if I want to really spoil someone, I will make little *choux* and fill them with pastry cream—chocolate, vanilla, or coffee. Then I will suddenly appear at the pool with a dozen, as a treat for the kids, or greet a visiting friend with a platter. These little cloud-like pastries will lift anyone's mood.

***

MAKE THE PUFFS. Preheat the oven to 400°F/200°C. Line a baking sheet with parchment paper.

In a medium saucepan, combine the milk, water, butter, granulated sugar, and salt and bring to a low boil over medium heat. Take off the heat, add the flour all at once, and mix with a wooden spoon until the dough is smooth.

Return to the heat for 1 minute, stirring constantly, to dry the dough slightly. The dough should be forming a ball. Remove from the heat and add the eggs one at a time, mixing well after each one so you have a smooth dough.

Transfer the dough to a pastry bag fitted with a medium plain tip, about ½ inch/1.3 cm in diameter. Pipe little mounds about the size of a golf ball onto the baking sheet, making sure to leave 1 inch/2.5 cm between them. Gently smooth and round the tops with the back of a teaspoon dipped in water.

Bake the *choux* until golden brown and puffed, about 25 minutes. Transfer to a wire rack to cool.

Meanwhile, make the coffee cream. In a medium saucepan, bring the milk and vanilla bean and seeds to a low boil over medium heat. In a bowl, whisk together the egg yolks, sugar, flour, and cornstarch.

MAKES 25 TO
30 SMALL PUFFS

For the puffs

½ cup/125 ml whole milk

½ cup (120 ml) water

7 tablespoons/105 g unsalted butter

1½ teaspoons granulated sugar

Pinch of fine sea salt

1 cup/120 g all-purpose flour, sifted

4 large eggs

For the coffee cream

2 cups/475 ml whole milk

½ vanilla bean, split lengthwise, seeds scraped out, seeds and bean reserved

4 large egg yolks

⅓ cup plus 2 tablespoons/80 g granulated sugar

Scant ¼ cup/30 g all-purpose flour

2 tablespoons/15 g cornstarch

2 tablespoons/30 g unsalted butter, cut into small cubes

4 teaspoons instant coffee granules

Confectioners' sugar for dusting

Slowly pour the hot milk into the egg yolk mixture, whisking constantly and very fast to prevent curdling. Pour the mixture back into the saucepan and whisk constantly over low heat until the mixture starts to thicken. Continue to whisk for 1 more minute, until the cream has thickened, then take off the heat and whisk in the butter and instant coffee.

Transfer to a bowl, press a piece of plastic wrap directly against the pastry cream to prevent a skin from forming, and let cool completely. Refrigerate until the cream is cold and thick enough for piping, at least 4 hours.

Just before serving, spoon the coffee cream into a pastry bag fitted with a small plain tip. Make a small slit in the base of each puff with a knife and pipe the coffee cream into the puffs. Sprinkle with confectioners' sugar and serve immediately.

HAZELNUT BLANCMANGE

I have a passion for medieval dishes, and blancmange is one of them. It was originally a dish made with shredded boiled chicken mixed into an almond milk–flavored liquid. The dish survived the dark days and has since become a chilled creamy dessert, most often still made with almonds. Hazelnuts, in my opinion, improve the flavor even further.

IN A FOOD PROCESSOR, blend the 1 cup/150 g hazelnuts with the milk for a minute or two, until the hazelnuts are ground. Pour into a bowl and set aside for 15 minutes so the flavors can develop.

Meanwhile, add 2 tablespoons warm water to the powdered gelatin and set aside to soften. Or, if using gelatin sheets, soak them in a bowl of cold water until softened; drain well before using.

Strain the hazelnut liquid through a sieve into a medium saucepan. Whisk in the ½ cup/120 ml cream and the sugar and, still whisking, bring to a low boil over medium-low heat, then cook just until the cream starts to thicken slightly. Remove from the heat.

Add the softened gelatin to the hot cream mixture and whisk until the gelatin is entirely dissolved. Set aside to cool.

Lightly oil a 9-inch/23-inch round cake pan or four to six ramekins.

Whip the remaining scant cup/225 ml heavy cream in a medium bowl until it holds stiff peaks. Gently fold in the hazelnut mixture. Pour into the pan and let set in the refrigerator for at least 8 hours, or overnight.

To serve, if using a cake pan, unmold the blancmange onto a serving plate and spoon out individual portions.

SERVES 4 TO 6

1 cup/150 g blanched hazelnuts, plus 10 nuts for garnish

1 cup/250 ml whole milk

1½ tablespoons powdered gelatin or 4 gelatin sheets

Scant 1½ cups/ 350 ml heavy cream

¾ cup/150 g granulated sugar

Vegetable oil for the pan

PISTACHIO SABAYON *with* STRAWBERRIES *and* MERINGUES

This was inspired by Fontaine de Mars, one of my favorite restaurants in Paris. We lived just around the corner, said hello to the staff every day, and loved to take the entire family there for a birthday dinner or a little Saturday night feast—and still do, if we are in town. In the summer months, they usually have this amazing dessert, a *coupe* filled with vanilla ice cream, strawberries, whipped cream, and pistachio sabayon. I always order it, no matter how much I have eaten; it's a must. I never asked for the recipe, but this is my homemade version, and I simply love it.

MAKE THE MERINGUES. Preheat the oven to 225°F/110°C.

Using an electric mixer, whip the egg whites in a large clean bowl (make sure it is free of any trace of oil), until they hold medium peaks. Add the salt and continue to whip, adding the granulated sugar about 2 tablespoons at a time, then whip until the whites are stiff and glossy. Tint with food coloring, if desired, to get a soft pink.

Line a baking sheet with parchment paper. Put the confectioners' sugar in a sifter or strainer and lightly dust the parchment with the sugar. You can use a small spoon to scoop the meringues. Or if you prefer the classic meringue shape, transfer the meringue to a piping bag fitted with a ½-inch/1.3-cm star tip. Pipe about 30 small meringues onto the baking sheet, leaving a little space between them.

Bake for 1½ hours for meringues that are still a little soft in the middle, or 2 hours for meringues that are dry throughout. Transfer to a wire rack to cool.

SERVES 6

For the meringues

4 large egg whites, at room temperature

A small pinch of fine sea salt

⅔ cup/130 g granulated sugar

A few drops of red food coloring (optional)

1 cup/120 g confectioners' sugar

For the pistachio sabayon

6 large egg yolks

⅔ cup/130 g granulated sugar

¼ cup/60 g dry Marsala wine

2 tablespoons pistachio paste (see Note, page 285), to taste

1 cup/240 ml heavy cream

1 pound/450 g small strawberries, hulled

½ cup/75 g slivered almonds (optional), toasted

Shortly before serving, make the sabayon. Fill a medium saucepan with 2 inches/5 cm of water and bring to a simmer. In a heatproof bowl, whisk together the egg yolks, granulated sugar, and Marsala until smooth. Mix in the pistachio paste. Put the bowl over the saucepan and whisk until the sabayon has thickened, about 4 to 5 minutes. Remove from the heat. The sabayon should be served within 15 minutes.

Whip the cream until it holds stiff peaks. I don't add sugar because I find the meringues have all the sweetness I need.

To serve, place the miniature meringues in dessert bowls, about 5 per bowl. Spoon 2 tablespoons whipped cream on top of each serving, add a small handful of strawberries, and pour pistachio sabayon over everything. Garnish with toasted almond slivers, if desired.

APRICOT PANNA COTTA

Panna cotta, the creamy Italian dessert, now appears on the menu in many French cafés, just as if it had always been there. Of course, we apply our own touches on this side of the border; this version with apricots is my favorite. A perfect panna cotta needs to be light and smooth but just firm enough to set; it mustn't be too jellified. And you should be able to really taste the cream and vanilla and, in this case, the fruit.

MAKE THE PANNA COTTA. Add the warm water to the powdered gelatin and set aside to soften. Or, if using gelatin sheets, soak them in a bowl of cold water until softened; drain well before using.

In a saucepan, combine the milk, cream, and sugar and bring to a simmer over medium heat, stirring to dissolve the sugar. Add the vanilla seeds and salt and remove the pan from the heat. Whisk in the gelatin until fully dissolved. Cover and set aside for 10 minutes.

Fill eight 4-ounce / 120-ml ramekins three-quarters full with the cream mixture. Let cool, then refrigerate for at least 6 hours, or, even better, overnight.

Make the apricot compote. Combine the apricots, water, sugar, star anise, and lemon juice in a medium saucepan, set the pan over medium-low heat, and bring to a soft, bubbly boil. Lower the heat and simmer until the apricots are very soft, 20 minutes. Set aside to cool. (The compote will keep for several days, covered, in the refrigerator.)

To serve, scoop 1 or 2 tablespoons of apricot compote onto each panna cotta.

SERVES 8

For the panna cotta

1 tablespoon plus 2½ teaspoons powdered gelatin or 5 gelatin sheets

2 tablespoons warm water

3¼ cups / 750 ml milk

1 cup / 250 ml heavy cream

⅔ cup / 150 g granulated sugar

1 vanilla bean, split lengthwise, seeds scraped out and reserved

A pinch of fine sea salt

For the apricot compote

1 pound / 450 g apricots, halved and pitted

3 tablespoons water

½ cup / 100 g granulated sugar

1 star anise

Juice of 1 lemon

CHILLED WHITE PEACHES IN WHITE WINE SYRUP

I can't think of another fruit that signifies summer as well as peaches, at least here in France. They are just about everywhere we go, fragrant, alluring, and, happily, reasonably priced. Peaches go fast in a big family, but there are times, especially on very hot days, when it feels as if the heat will catch up with all of us and spoil the peaches. On days like that, the solution to all our problems is making this refreshing dessert, to save the peaches—and ourselves.

BRING A MEDIUM POT of water to a boil. Plunge the peaches into the boiling water for 10 seconds. Remove with a slotted spoon and peel them. Cut in half and remove the pits.

In a large saucepan, combine the sugar, wine, cinnamon, vanilla bean and seeds, lemon zest, and lemon juice. Bring to a boil over medium heat, stirring to dissolve the sugar. Add the halved peaches and cook for 3 minutes, just to soften the peaches slightly. Transfer to a bowl and set aside to cool in the syrup.

Sprinkle the cooled peaches with the mint leaves, cover, and refrigerate until cold, at least 3 hours.

Serve the peaches drizzled with their syrup.

SERVES 6 TO 8

8 white peaches

1½ cups / 300 g granulated sugar

¾ cup / 180 ml white wine

1 cinnamon stick

1 vanilla bean, split lengthwise, seeds scraped out, seeds and bean reserved

Grated zest and juice of 1 lemon

A small handful of fresh mint leaves

AUTUMN

It was our first real fall here in Médoc and we were excited about the prospect of finding cèpes. We had bought porcini mushrooms in markets in Paris, at the cost of an arm and a leg, and the thought of foraging for our own in the nearby woods sounded charming and adventurous.

A few mornings later, I set out to look for the mushrooms with a basket large enough to carry at least a dozen big ones, only to come home hours later with an empty basket. My husband took the dogs for long walks in the rain and he, too, came up short. Then one day he proudly brought home a very big, soggy mushroom and placed it on the dining table. The whole family huddled around. It looked ugly and wet, not like the beautiful cèpes of my dreams, but perhaps we could still cook it? Nobody really seemed to want that, but we didn't want to admit that it was no good either. Later that evening, a worm crawled out of the mushroom, and seconds later the cèpe flew out the window; I wasn't going to cook anything with worms in it.

In November, when we celebrated my daughter's birthday, one of her friends' mothers was boasting about the countless kilos of cèpes she had found in October. She asked if we had frozen ours. It was tempting to say yes, but the truth prevailed and I said that where we lived there simply hadn't been any this year. She seemed surprised, and when they were leaving, she took a little walk in the garden and almost immediately returned with a mushroom. We laughed hard—it was embarrassing but mostly funny. I did, however, decide that this would not happen again.

The next fall, I kept my eyes and ears open. A hushed conversation at the greengrocer's marked the start of the season for me. The merchant and a customer were talking in subdued voices. "So did you find any?" he asked. "Just a couple small ones," said the customer, adding, "I heard that Madame X found bags' worth this weekend." The merchant peered at him seriously, then looked in my direction, sensing I was in on the conversation, and said, "That's normal, she's a mushroom witch."

When I left the store, I had one thing on my mind—I too would become a witch of the forest. I was so determined to succeed that I ventured into parts of the woods I had never been before, stung myself on countless plants, got lost, and even got a bit scared, but my commitment never wavered.

One morning I set out as usual, but this time I did not return empty-handed. I found my first real cèpe, so beautiful and pure, partially covered by moist, decaying leaves. It seemed a shame to cook it, so I decided to slice it thin and serve it raw as a carpaccio, with a little olive oil, for lunch. Later that day I returned to the forest and that time came home with close to a dozen. It was as if the floodgates had opened,

and suddenly there were cèpes everywhere. My conjuring powers even extended to my family, who also started finding cèpes all around.

At first the cèpes graced our big kitchen table, taking their place in the ever-changing still life next to the figs and pumpkins. But after a while, even our appetites could no longer keep up with our hunting prowess and the mushrooms started finding their way straight from forest to freezer. Although I always feel it's something of a shame to treat them that way, in winter, when I bring them back to life, the flavor they add to my sauces and soups returns me to the forest.

Cooking is always a pleasure for me, but my favorite culinary time of the year has to be autumn. The produce is richer, grander than at any other time. On a cool, dark night, I'll sometimes be standing by the stove, candlelight flickering in the room, beautiful food laid out all around me, pumpkins, mushrooms, nuts. I might be cooking something with cèpes or snails, calves' liver, or even pears drenched in red wine, adding herbs and broths, simmering and stirring. At times like those, making dinner feels like something akin to sorcery and I sense a deep connection to everyone who has cooked mysterious and delicious food in their little cabins in the forest.

Autumn really is the season of the witch.

STARTERS

Pumpkin Soup

Harvest Soup

Cèpe and Parsley Tartlets

Escargots à la Bordelaise

Gambas Flambées with Pastis

Foie Gras Terrine with Armagnac

MAIN COURSES
AND SIDES

Coquilles St.-Jacques with Braised Endive

Quail Grilled over Grapevines

Squab Pie with Foie Gras and Armagnac

Seared Foie Gras with Grapes and Figs

Grilled Entrecôte à la Bordelaise

Slow-Cooked Lamb with Croquant Ratatouille

Pork Cheek Ravioli with Cèpes

Potatoes à la Lyonnaise

Butternut Gratin

DESSERTS

Chocolate Meringue Swirls with Chocolate Sauce
and Crème Chantilly

Toulousaine Violet Meringues

Chocolate Tart

Calvados and Crème Fraîche Apple Tart

Apple Tart with Orange Flower Water

Galette Pérougienne

Pears à la Médocaine

Crêpes with Salted-Butter Caramel

PUMPKIN SOUP

In autumn and winter, we always have lots of pumpkins in the house, and even if we are all stocked up, I often can't resist bringing more home from the market. I also often receive them as gifts, so you can imagine the mountain of pumpkins that piles up in October. I roast them, make a mash out of them, use them in salads. The most popular pumpkin dish I make is this soup; it's a firm favorite with the kids. I try my best to cook healthy food for my family, and serving this soup always makes me feel like a good mom.

IN A LARGE POT, heat the olive oil over medium heat. Add the shallots and garlic and cook until lightly golden, 4 to 5 minutes. Add the pumpkin and parsnips, season with salt and pepper, and cook for 8 minutes.

Pour in the milk and vegetable stock and bring to a boil. Lower the heat, cover, and simmer until the vegetables are tender, 15 to 20 minutes.

Purée the soup in batches in a blender, adding a little bit of milk or water if the soup is on the thick side. Season with salt and pepper.

Mix together the crème fraîche, walnuts, and chives.

Divide the soup among bowls and top each with a spoonful of the crème fraîche mixture and a sprinkling of chives.

SERVES 4 TO 6

2 tablespoons extra-virgin olive oil

6 shallots, thinly sliced

3 garlic cloves, thinly sliced

1⅓ pounds / 600 g pumpkin, peeled, seeded, and roughly chopped

5 ounces / 150 g parsnips, peeled and chopped

Fine sea salt and freshly ground black pepper

2 cups / 475 ml whole milk, or more if needed

1¼ cups / 300 ml vegetable stock

¾ cup / 180 ml crème fraîche

⅓ cup / 60 g walnuts, coarsely chopped

A few fresh chives, finely chopped, plus more for serving

HARVEST SOUP

This is a typical Médocain soup, perfect after a long, hard day's work in the vineyards during harvest season. I was invited one day to a friend's château, and this wholesome soup was bubbling away in a huge cast-iron pot in his kitchen. *Soupe des vendanges* started in the vineyard kitchens, and it was traditionally filled with enough meat to feed an entire village. It is eaten with copious amounts of bread, and the meat is served separately, with cornichons, mustard, and a tomato. Every winemaking family has its own recipe, each full of vegetables; the key is to braise the meat as long as possible, rendering it *moelleux*, soft and tender. A nice glass of red wine, a crisp baguette, and this comforting soup is a good way to welcome autumn.

MAKE THE SOUP. Put the beef in a large pot and add just enough water to cover. Bring to a boil over medium heat and skim off the scum that floats to the surface. Add the potatoes, carrots, turnips, cabbage, onion, leek, celery, garlic, bouquet garni, and salt and pepper to taste and bring to a boil, then lower the heat, cover, and simmer until the beef is completely tender, 3 to 4 hours. Add water if needed to keep the beef submerged.

Meanwhile, prepare the garnish. In a small bowl, mix together the tomatoes, parsley, garlic, and olive oil. Season with salt and pepper.

Remove the beef from the soup and put it on a cutting board. Cut into slices and transfer to a serving plate. Ladle the broth and vegetables into bowls. Top each with a spoonful of the tomato garnish. Serve the meat on the side, along with cornichons and mustard. And lots of sliced baguettes to dip in the soup.

SERVES 6

For the soup

2.2 pounds / 1 kg beef shoulder or shin

10 ounces / 300 g russet potatoes, peeled and diced

10 ounces / 300 g carrots, peeled and diced

10 ounces / 300 g turnips, peeled and diced

½ cabbage, coarsely chopped

1 onion, finely chopped

1 leek, white part only, thinly sliced

1 celery stalk, finely chopped

5 garlic cloves, thinly sliced

1 bouquet garni (see page 159)

Fine sea salt and freshly ground black pepper

For the garnish

12 ounces / 340 g
    tomatoes, peeled,
    halved, seeded, and
    diced

A bunch of fresh
    parsley, leaves
    removed and finely
    chopped

1 garlic clove, minced

2 teaspoons extra-
    virgin olive oil

Fine sea salt and
    freshly ground black
    pepper

Cornichons

Dijon mustard

Baguettes

BOUQUET GARNI

Some of my favorite moments in the kitchen include
assembling herbs into an aromatic bouquet, tying them
together with string, and then dropping them into whatever
broth or stew they are meant to enhance. If garlic and wine
are the tastes of France, then a bouquet garni must be its
perfume; it's a staple in any French kitchen. The assortment
of herbs must, as far as I am concerned, always include a bay
leaf or two and plenty of thyme; sometimes I add a sprig of
sage or rosemary, a bit of parsley for freshness, or oregano if
I have it. It's traditional to wrap everything in a piece of leek
green, but truthfully I only do this when I have one handy.
When the bouquet garni has given all its aroma to a soup or a
sauce, it can be easily fished out and discarded.

CÈPE *and* PARSLEY TARTLETS

Cèpes, or porcini, are a major theme here in Médoc. As soon as the season starts, I am off in the wee hours, dressed in combat clothing, ready for an adventure in the forest. You have to follow your intuition, have a good sense of smell, and look for clues. The mushrooms are often found near oak trees, although you can't always count on that. Nothing beats the feeling of coming back home, covered in earth, ferns, and scratches, with a basket filled with cèpes, which would cost a small fortune in Paris. That said, since everyone does not live in Médoc, this recipe can be made with any fresh mushrooms, preferably wild.

8 ounces / 230 g puff pastry, homemade (page 28) or store-bought, defrosted if frozen

4 tablespoons / 60 g unsalted butter

1 large shallot, finely chopped

3 garlic cloves, finely chopped

1⅓ pounds / 580 g fresh cèpes (porcini), sliced in half

Fine sea salt and freshly ground black pepper

A bunch of fresh parsley, leaves removed and finely chopped

Extra-virgin olive oil for drizzling

PREHEAT THE OVEN to 350°F / 180°C.

Prepare the pastry. On a lightly floured surface, roll out the pastry to ¼ inch / 0.5 cm thick. Cut out four 4½-inch / 11.5-cm circles with a pastry cutter or knife. Prick the pastry circles all over with a fork, arrange on a parchment-lined baking sheet, and cover with another piece of parchment paper. To prevent the pastry from puffing up too much, place another baking sheet on top.

Bake for 10 minutes. Remove the weight and second sheet of parchment paper, return the pastry to the oven, and bake until golden, 6 to 7 minutes more. Transfer to individual plates.

While the pastry is baking, melt the butter in a sauté pan over medium heat. Add the shallot and garlic and cook until soft, 1 to 2 minutes. Turn the heat to high, add the cèpes, and season with salt and pepper. Cook until lightly golden, 2 to 3 minutes.

Divide the cèpes among the pastry circles and sprinkle with the parsley. Drizzle with a bit of olive oil and serve immediately.

ESCARGOTS À LA BORDELAISE

I grew up on the classic Burgundy dish of snails in parsley and garlic with butter and I never really thought of making them any other way. But here in Bordeaux, they love, for obvious reasons, to add wine to everything and then call it "à la Bordelaise." I'm lucky enough to have some snail farmers, the Pions, as friends and neighbors, and while she loves them the Burgundy way, he's more of a Bordelaise guy. They were generous enough to share their recipe with me some years ago and it's something we love to have in autumn when there is an abundance of snails. While it's in many ways a fairly traditional ragoût, with ham, sausage, tomatoes, and wine, the snails give it a very different kind of meaty flavor. I always make lots of extra sauce and freeze it, then serve it over pasta when the mood strikes me.

IN A LARGE SAUCEPAN, heat the olive oil over medium heat. Add the shallots and garlic and cook until soft and slightly golden, about 3 minutes. Add the sausage, ham, and parsley and cook, stirring, until the meat is browned, 5 to 6 minutes.

Take the pan off the heat, add the flour, and mix well. Return to the heat, add the tomato purée, and mix well. Bring to a simmer, cover, and simmer over low heat for 15 minutes.

Add the chicken stock, red wine, and piment d'Espelette and season with salt and pepper. Bring to a simmer, cover, and simmer for 15 minutes.

Add the snails and cook over very low heat for 10 minutes. Serve immediately.

SERVES 4

3 tablespoons extra-virgin olive oil

3 shallots, minced

2 garlic cloves, minced

1 pound / 450 g sausage meat

5 ounces / 150 g ham, diced

A handful of chopped fresh parsley

1 tablespoon all-purpose flour

4 cups / 1 liter tomato purée

2 cups / 475 ml chicken stock

2 cups / 475 ml dry red wine

A pinch of piment d'Espelette or mild chile powder

Fine sea salt and freshly ground black pepper

9 dozen cooked (shelled) snails (canned are fine)

WINE

Wine exists for two reasons: to drink and to cook with (well, and to drink while you cook with it). I was going to say that the first reason is the most important one and then I changed my mind. Twice. The whole practice of browning meat in a pan and then deglazing the tasty bits would be so much less tasty without wine. The sauces I like the most have wine in them; it deepens the flavor of any dish.

There is no reason to cook with expensive wine; a simple but drinkable bottle will usually do. Bear in mind, though, that a bad one might spoil your cooking. I tend to cook with wine that costs around 4 to 5 euros a bottle.

GAMBAS FLAMBÉES *with* PASTIS

Médoc is a wonderful mixture of châteaus and seaside towns. All year round, locals drink wine and eat oysters. In autumn and winter, they hunt and forage for mushrooms, and in summer, everybody has *gambas*, jumbo prawns. People gather for little *gambas* feasts, wonderfully rustic and messy affairs; peeling the prawns is not always easy, but that's half the fun. Some use whiskey or Cognac to flambé their *gambas*, but the anise flavor that pastis lends wins out for me every time. French fries, for dipping into the sauce, are a must.

IN A LARGE SAUTÉ PAN, heat the olive oil over medium heat. Add the shallots and garlic and cook until softened, about 3 minutes. Raise the heat to high, add the prawns, and cook, turning once, until opaque throughout, 3 to 4 minutes.

Add the pastis. Light a match and carefully ignite the cooking liquid to flambé the prawns, shaking the pan briskly until the flame dies out. Pour in the white wine and simmer to reduce for 2 to 3 minutes.

Add the tomatoes, season with salt and pepper, and stir all of the ingredients together. Lower the heat to medium, swirl in the butter, and sprinkle in the piment d'Espelette. The sauce should be glossy and the prawns cooked through.

Transfer to a large serving dish and sprinkle the chives on top.

SERVES 4

- 2 tablespoons extra-virgin olive oil
- 2 shallots, thinly sliced
- 2 garlic cloves, thinly sliced
- 2 pounds / 900 g medium head-on jumbo prawns, rinsed
- 2 tablespoons pastis or other anise-flavored liquor
- 3 tablespoons dry white wine
- 20 cherry tomatoes, halved
- Fine sea salt and freshly ground black pepper
- 2 tablespoons unsalted butter
- ¼ teaspoon piment d'Espelette
- A small bunch of fresh chives, finely chopped

FOIE GRAS TERRINE
with ARMAGNAC

I am a real foie gras fan and always have been. When I was growing up in Hong Kong, it was the food that perhaps most reminded me of France. We'd have it from time to time in French restaurants there and all the time at my grandmother's house in Moissac. And whenever we were invited to houses of my mother's childhood friends, inevitably they would serve their own home-made *terrine de foie gras*; in the Sud-Ouest, everybody has geese.

In Médoc, I like to serve foie gras with figs on toast when we have guests. It's so easy to make and, may I say it, economical there. In Paris, my local charcuterie made a dreamy *foie gras maison* with Armagnac in it, so I add some to mine, too. An elegant way of serving foie gras is on *pain d'epice* (spice bread) with a glass of Sauternes; while I like it that way, my favorite way to eat it is on toasted Poilâne sourdough bread, sprinkled with salt and pepper, with well-chilled Champagne.

FILL A BOWL with ice water and add 1 tablespoon of the coarse salt. Soak the foie gras in the water for 2 hours, turning it from time to time and replenishing the ice if need be. Drain and pat dry.

Preheat the oven to 155°F / 70°C.

Line a work surface with parchment paper. Gently separate the 2 lobes of the foie gras. Using the tip of a sharp paring knife, remove any veins and nerves along with greenish or bloody bits. It is important to remove all the unwanted parts, so don't worry if you are deconstructing the foie gras too much. It will all be pressed together in the terrine mold, so that won't matter.

SERVES 8 TO 10

2 tablespoons coarse sea salt

One 1⅓-pound / 580-g good-quality fresh duck organic foie gras

1 teaspoon freshly ground black pepper

1 tablespoon Armagnac

Split the foie gras lobes and season on all sides with the remaining 1 table-spoon of salt and the pepper. Sprinkle the Armagnac all over. Layer the foie gras into a 3½ × 15½-inch/9 × 14-cm ceramic terrine mold, pressing on the foie gras with the back of a spoon so there is no trapped air. Cover with the terrine lid.

Put the terrine mold in a small roasting pan and fill the roasting pan with enough boiling water to reach halfway up the side of the terrine mold. Bake for 45 minutes. Take the foie gras out of the oven, remove from the water, and let cool for 5 hours.

Remove the excess fat from the top of the foie gras, spooning it into a small bowl, then refrigerate. When the fat has slightly hardened, scoop just enough of it over the foie gras to seal the terrine. Refrigerate, covered, for at least 24 hours before serving. (You can keep the foie gras in the refrigerator for at least 10 days.)

Slice and serve slightly chilled.

COQUILLES ST.-JACQUES
with BRAISED ENDIVE

This recipe is a case study in what a little butter can do. Cooking the scallops (*coquilles St.-Jacques*) in sizzling butter unleashes a hundred sophisticated flavors, yet when you taste them, you almost feel as if you cheated because the dish was so simple to make. I can't think of a better example of minimal input, maximum reward. The same happens to the endives, which are transformed from bitter to sweet. Eaten on its own, each part is delicious, but combine them, and sparks fly. I like to enjoy this dish with a glass of chilled white Burgundy; it makes for a very happy threesome.

IN A LARGE SAUTÉ PAN, melt 4 tablespoons / 55 g of the butter over medium-high heat. Cook the endive until tender, about 4 minutes. Season with salt and pepper, reduce the heat to low, cover the pan, and cook the endive until very tender, 10 to 15 minutes.

Meanwhile, heat the remaining 4 tablespoons / 55 g butter in another large sauté pan over medium-high heat. Pat the scallops dry with paper towels and season with salt and pepper on both sides. When the butter starts to sizzle, add the scallops to the pan and sear them until golden brown and barely cooked through, 2 to 3 minutes per side.

Serve the scallops on top of the braised endive, sprinkled with the chives.

SERVES 4

8 tablespoons / 1 stick / 110 g unsalted butter

5 Belgian endives, separated into leaves

Fine sea salt and freshly ground black pepper

16 large sea scallops, side muscle removed

A small bunch of fresh chives, finely chopped

QUAIL GRILLED
over GRAPEVINES

When temperatures cool and leaves start falling, I often plan one last outdoor feast with friends and neighbors. There is something so romantic about a fall dinner outside, everyone wearing sweaters or shawls but still looking healthy and tanned from summer. I decorate the table with pumpkins, apples, and pears and everyone brings bottles of great wine. We gather in the house and have a glass of wine, then carry tables, baskets filled with food, and chairs out into the woods. Someone hangs the lanterns, someone else sets up the fire, and it begins. We might have pumpkin soup to start, and a Pérougienne cake for dessert, but we always have quails *à la broche* for the main course.

Once temperatures dip even further, I frequently roast the quail in my oven, prepared in a similar way—wrapped in bacon, stuffed with herbs and garlic—and they are always delicious.

PREPARE A MEDIUM-HOT FIRE in a grill, preferably using dried grapevines.

Season the quail inside and out with salt and pepper. Put 1 teaspoon butter, 1 garlic clove, and 1 rosemary sprig in the cavity of each quail. Wrap a slice of pork belly around each one and truss the birds with kitchen twine to secure the pork. Drizzle with the olive oil. Insert a metal skewer horizontally through 2 birds, side by side. Repeat with the other 2 birds.

When the branches (or coals) have ashed over, put the skewered birds on the grill and cook, turning occasionally, until cooked through (the juices should run clear, not pink, when you prick a thigh with a knife), about 20 minutes. Serve immediately.

SERVES 4

4 quail, cleaned

Fine sea salt and freshly ground black pepper

4 teaspoons unsalted butter

4 garlic cloves

4 small sprigs of fresh rosemary

4 thin slices noir de Bigorre pork belly, pancetta, or bacon

¼ cup / 60 ml extra-virgin olive oil for drizzling

A REAL BUTCHER

A man and his wife are standing in front of the butcher counter, discussing what to cook for Easter. Lamb, of course, but a shoulder or a leg? The butcher thinks a leg is best; the wife is more comfortable with a shoulder. The husband doesn't want to contradict his wife, but maybe the butcher knows best? He is, after all, the butcher. They take so much time you'd think they were buying a car or a computer. And then, when they reach a decision and you start edging hopefully toward the counter, your own order practically spilling from your lips, they start discussing another meal, something even more complicated. Then you realize you'll be there for a while.

Buying meat is serious business in France and, all inconvenience aside, that's probably how it should be. We are, after all, talking about meat, something that used to be a live animal. I like to know where my meat comes from; I like to know that the animal was well treated. And so I don't mind waiting.

A good butcher, like Monsieur Manenti, knows not only how to buy and cut good meat, but also how to handle people. He listens attentively, yet has his own strong opinion. There is a right way to do things, and he knows it. He can be consulted about various recipes, and while he may not be the most creative cook, he can tell you exactly how long a certain cut of pork should be cooked. Once I threw a dinner party and served Hong Shao Pork (page 294). It was a great success, and when I visited my butcher some days later and told him how happy I was with his meat, he had a smile on his face. My guests, all of them his clients, had visited his shop after the dinner and had praised the meal. He was part of that success and was rightfully basking in the praise.

SEARED FOIE GRAS
with GRAPES *and* FIGS

My mother was born and raised in Moissac, a little town near Toulouse in southwest France that's known for two things: its famous cloister and its incredible Chasselas grapes. Small, round, almost translucent, and utterly fabulous, they may be the best grapes in the world. Whenever I would see them in August and September at the market in Paris, I'd feel happy and a bit proud; sometimes I would even tell the vendors, "These are my grandmother's grapes." The Sud-Ouest region in general is the heartland of foie gras and the home of all things duck. While I don't have *foie gras poêlée* very often, when I do, I want to do it right. And that means with Chasselas grapes and figs. This dish just feels like autumn to me.

HEAT A LARGE SAUTÉ PAN over high heat until very hot. Season the foie gras on both sides with salt and pepper and dust with flour to ensure a crisp exterior. Add the foie gras, figs, and grapes to the pan (do not add any fat, as the foie gras will release its own) and cook until the foie gras is browned but still very rosy in the middle, 1 minute on each side or less. Do not overcook.

Quickly add the Cognac, light a match, and carefully ignite the Cognac. Shake the pan until the flame dies out. Cook until golden, 3 minutes more. Serve immediately, with toasted country bread.

SERVES 4

One 1-pound/450-g good-quality fresh duck or goose foie gras, veins and nerves removed and cut into ½-inch/1.5-cm-thick slices

Fine sea salt and freshly ground black pepper

All-purpose flour for dusting

8 small fresh figs, stemmed and quartered

10 ounces/300 g Chasselas or other small green grapes

2 tablespoons/30 ml Cognac

Toasted slices of country bread

GRILLED ENTRECÔTE
À LA BORDELAISE

A big juicy entrecôte, or rib-eye steak, seasoned with just salt and pepper and cooked over high heat until crusty and juicy, has always had a special place in my heart. Frankly, I didn't think it could be improved on—that is, until I moved to Médoc. As you may be well aware of at this point, the people of Bordeaux love adding shallots to everything. Here they work wonders and really complement the flavor of the meat. Add a bit of bone marrow, and you are in meat heaven. It's fine to cook this entrecôte on a regular grill, but if you want the full Bordelaise effect, I recommend adding dried grapevines to the fire so that a hint of Cabernet or Merlot finds its way into your steak. Having this dish without a glass of red wine is a crime!

SERVES 2

4 beef marrow bones

One 1-pound /
   400- to 500-g rib-eye
   steak

   Fine sea salt and
   freshly ground black
   pepper

6 shallots, finely
   chopped

PREHEAT THE OVEN to 400°F/200°C.

To remove the marrow from the bones, put the bones in a baking dish and bake until the marrow is soft enough to scrape out of the bones, 10 to 15 minutes.

Prepare a medium-hot fire in a grill. You can add dried grapevines, if desired (to increase the smoky flavor).

Season the meat with salt and pepper. Grill the steak until browned and cooked to medium-rare, 3 to 4 minutes per side.

Heat the blade of a knife over the grill and spread the bone marrow over the meat. Sprinkle the shallots all over. Remove from the grill and serve immediately.

SLOW-COOKED LAMB *with* CROQUANT RATATOUILLE

Ratatouille with lamb is a classic French pairing. Of course, ratatouille doesn't have to be paired with anything at all—except perhaps a fried egg, some good bread, and a glass of rosé. But for a big festive meal, ratatouille is only too happy to share the stage with slices of juicy lamb.

For a long time, I made ratatouille in the simplest, most old-fashioned way, and if I wanted a change, I simply made a vegetable tian (see page 103). That was until I met Gilles de Marcellius, the charming caretaker of Château Ormes de Pez, and added his way of making ratatouille (and roasting lamb) to my repertoire. Although the ingredients are the same, his refined approach leads to a very different outcome; the vegetables retain a bit of texture and crunch (which is why I call this crouquant) instead of practically dissolving into each other. These days it's my preferred version. Meeting interesting new people is one of the best things in life, and when they give you good recipes, you remember them forever.

PREHEAT THE OVEN 275°F/140°C.

In a large Dutch oven or other heavy pot, heat the butter and olive oil over medium heat. Season the lamb with salt and pepper. Add the lamb to the pot and brown on all sides, 3 to 4 minutes per side. Remove the meat from the pot and set aside.

Toss the carrot, onion, celery, tomato, and garlic into the pot and season with salt and pepper. Sauté the vegetables for 2 minutes. Return the meat and any juices to the pot. Add enough water to come halfway up the sides

(recipe continues)

2 tablespoons unsalted butter

2 tablespoons extra-virgin olive oil

One 2-pound / 1-kg boneless lamb shoulder roast, tied

Fine sea salt and freshly ground black pepper

1 large carrot, peeled and roughly chopped

1 onion, roughly chopped

1 celery stalk, roughly chopped

1 tomato, roughly chopped

6 garlic cloves, unpeeled

1 bay leaf

A few sprigs each of fresh thyme and rosemary

Croquant Ratatouille (recipe follows)

of the meat, season the water with salt and pepper, and add the bay leaf. Bring to a boil, then remove from the heat. Lay the sprigs of thyme and rosemary on top of the meat.

Cover the pot and transfer to the oven. Cook for 6 to 7 hours, checking on the meat every 2 hours and basting it with some of the cooking liquid. The meat is done when it is so tender you can pull off a piece with a fork.

Slice the meat and serve with the vegetables, drizzling the cooking liquid over all, with the ratatouille on the side.

NOTE: *To make a sauce, strain the cooking liquid into a saucepan. Add 1¾ cups/400 ml stock, preferably lamb or veal, and a small glass of white wine, and simmer to reduce by half. Check the seasoning and then pass the sauce through a sieve into a bowl. Drizzle the sauce over the lamb before serving.*

CROQUANT RATATOUILLE

BRING A LARGE POT of water to a boil over medium-high heat. Add the tomatoes and blanch until the skin starts to crack, 1 to 2 minutes. Drain, then peel, halve, and seed the tomatoes. Keeping each vegetable separate, dice the tomatoes, eggplant, zucchini, red and green peppers, and onions into small cubes.

In a large sauté pan, heat a few tablespoons of olive oil over medium heat. Add the onions, garlic, thyme, and bay leaf, season with salt and pepper, and sauté until the onions are softened but still crunchy, about 3 minutes. Scoop the onions into a bowl. Add a little more olive oil to the pan and repeat with the remaining vegetables in this order, returning the garlic, thyme, and bay leaf to the pan each time: peppers, eggplant, zucchini, and tomatoes.

Finally, combine all of the ingredients together in the pan and mix well. Serve, or cover with a lid and set aside until serving time, up to 6 hours. Reheat over medium heat for 3 to 4 minutes before serving.

SERVES 4 TO 6

5 large tomatoes

2 medium eggplant

2 large zucchini

2 red bell peppers

2 green bell peppers

2 white onions

About ⅓ cup / 80 ml extra-virgin olive oil

2 garlic cloves, crushed and peeled

A few sprigs of fresh thyme

1 bay leaf

Fine sea salt and freshly ground black pepper

PORK CHEEK RAVIOLI
with CÈPES

I frequently make pasta at home, especially ravioli, usually with Italian-inspired stuffings and sauces. The filling in this one, though, is all French and I serve it with an equally French creamy wine sauce. It's a dish I like to make when I have some time, typically on a Saturday, with a bit of music in the background. The kids enjoy helping me roll out and cut the ravioli, then we fill them together and prepare a fine little feast.

START THE FILLING. In a medium pot, heat 1 tablespoon of the olive oil over medium heat. Brown the pork cheeks on both sides, about 5 minutes. Transfer to a plate.

Add another tablespoon of olive oil to the pot and cook the onion, carrot, and half of the garlic until lightly golden, 3 to 4 minutes. Return the pork cheeks to the pot, add the bouquet garni, and season with salt and pepper. Pour in the red wine and bring to a low simmer. Add water just to cover the meat. Cover with a lid, lower the heat, and simmer until the meat is very tender and falling apart, about 2 hours.

While the pork is cooking, make the pasta dough. Put the flour on a clean work surface and make a well in the center. Add the salt, eggs, and olive oil. Using a fork, mix the egg mixture, then gradually mix in the flour, using your hands when the dough is too stiff to stir. Then knead with the heels of your hands, sprinkling the dough with additional flour if it gets too sticky, until it is soft and elastic, but still slightly sticky, 6 to 8 minutes. Shape into a ball and wrap in plastic wrap. Let rest at room temperature for 30 minutes.

(recipe continues)

SERVES 6

For the filling and garnish

¼ cup / 60 ml extra-virgin olive oil

10 ounces / 300 g pork cheeks

1 small onion, finely chopped

1 small carrot, diced

1 garlic clove, minced

1 bouquet garni (see page 159)

Fine sea salt and freshly ground black pepper

¾ cup / 180 ml dry red wine

12 ounces / 340 g fresh cèpes (porcini)

1 shallot, minced

A handful of finely chopped fresh parsley

2 tablespoons / 30 g unsalted butter

2 tablespoons (or additional) port or red wine

2 tablespoons / 30 ml heavy cream

A handful of chopped fresh parsley

Continue with the filling. Cut half of the mushrooms—the nicest ones—into quarters and reserve for garnish. Thinly slice the remaining mushrooms.

Heat 1 tablespoon of the olive oil in a large sauté pan over high heat. Add the sliced mushrooms and season with salt and pepper, then add the shallot and the remaining garlic and cook until the mushrooms are slightly golden, 2 to 3 minutes. Sprinkle with the parsley and set aside to cool.

Drain the pork cheeks, reserving the broth, and transfer to a plate to cool for 10 minutes.

Transfer the pork cheeks to a food processor, add the cooked mushrooms and 4 to 5 tablespoons of the broth, and process for about 3 seconds to gently mix. Season with salt and pepper.

With a rolling pin, roll out the dough on a floured surface just until it is thin enough to fit through the rollers of a pasta machine. Using the pasta machine, roll the dough as thin as possible, starting with the widest setting and progressing to the thinnest one possible.

Cut the pasta into 3-inch/8-cm squares. Spoon 1 tablespoon pork cheek filling into the center of half of the squares. Moisten the edges of one square with water, top with another pasta square, and press the edges firmly together to seal, taking care not to include any air. Repeat with the remaining pasta squares. Cover the ravioli with a damp towel so they do not dry out.

Bring a large pot of salted water to a boil.

Meanwhile, cook the mushrooms for the garnish. In a large sauté pan, heat the remaining 1 tablespoon olive oil and 1 tablespoon of the butter over high heat. Cook the quartered mushrooms until lightly golden, about 30 seconds on each side. Season with salt and pepper and transfer to a plate.

Add the remaining 1 tablespoon butter to the pan and melt over medium heat. Add ½ cup/120 ml of the reserved pork broth and the port and simmer until the sauce has reduced and thickened, about 4 minutes. Reduce the heat, add the cream, and return the cèpes to the pan. Stir for 5 seconds to combine, then take off the heat. Keep warm.

Drop the ravioli into the boiling water and stir gently. The ravioli are cooked when they float to the surface, about 1½ minutes. Scoop out with a slotted spoon and transfer to warm shallow bowls. Top with the mushrooms and sauce, sprinkle with parsley, and serve immediately.

POTATOES À LA LYONNAISE

What can you say about a simple potato dish that goes with everything? That it's the little black dress of side dishes—but wouldn't that be a cliché? I think it's best to say that it is a dish I would happily welcome at my table anytime. I can't think of a meal that would not be improved if served alongside Lyonnaise potatoes. Frankly, as I am writing this, I realize I can't serve dinner tonight without these. That's how good they are.

PREHEAT THE OVEN to 350°F/180°C.

Put the potatoes in a large pot, add enough salted cold water to cover, bring to a boil, and cook until parboiled, 10 to 15 minutes. Drain in a colander and rinse under cool running water. Let cool for a few minutes, then slice the potatoes into ⅛-inch/3- to 4-mm-thick slices.

In a large sauté pan, melt 2 tablespoons of the butter. Add about one-quarter of the potatoes and fry, seasoning them with salt and pepper, until golden, about 6 minutes. Transfer to a plate. Continue frying the potatoes, adding more butter each time (you should use about 8 tablespoons/120 g in total), until all of them are cooked.

Meanwhile, in another sauté pan, heat the remaining 2 tablespoons/30 g butter over medium heat. Cook the onions until golden, about 5 minutes.

Return all of the potatoes to the pan, add the onions, and mix gently. Cook for 5 more minutes for the flavors to combine.

Transfer the potatoes and onions to a large baking dish. Bake until gently sizzling, about 10 minutes.

Sprinkle the parsley over the potatoes and serve.

SERVES 4

2 pounds/900 g new potatoes, peeled

About 11 tablespoons/ 150 g unsalted butter

Fine sea salt and freshly ground black pepper

2 onions, thinly sliced

A bunch of fresh parsley, leaves removed and finely chopped

BUTTERNUT GRATIN

I'm as fond as anyone of a simple steak frites dinner. Sometimes I make a Béarnaise sauce, but sometimes, especially if the wine is good, it's enough to serve the steak with just a spoonful of Dijon mustard. I always have some greens to go with it, steamed haricots verts or spinach or just a simple salad. Sometimes I have a small steak and lots of spinach. That's when my husband thinks I've read some article and I'm suddenly on a diet. But that would never happen. It's just that sometimes French fries are . . . well, not exactly what I am looking for, and then I need an alternative. If it's pumpkin season, this gratin is one of the best. Steak pairs really well with roasted squash, and this gratin version makes the duo even more satisfying.

3 tablespoons unsalted butter, plus more for the baking dish

1 large onion, thinly sliced

1 garlic clove, thinly sliced

1½ pounds / 680 g butternut squash (about 1 large), peeled, halved lengthwise, seeded, and thinly sliced

¼ teaspoon grated nutmeg

Fine sea salt and freshly ground black pepper

½ cup / 120 ml heavy cream

¾ cup / 45 g fresh bread crumbs

¾ cup / 75 g grated Comté cheese

A few fresh chives, finely chopped

PREHEAT THE OVEN to 350°F / 180°C. Butter a 10-inch / 25-cm baking dish.

In a large sauté pan, heat 2 tablespoons of the butter over medium heat. Add the onion and garlic and cook until soft and translucent, 4 minutes. Add the squash slices and nutmeg and cook until slightly tender, 3 to 5 minutes. Season with salt and pepper.

Transfer the squash mixture to the baking dish. Pour the cream all over, sprinkle the bread crumbs and cheese on top, and dot with the remaining 1 tablespoon butter.

Bake until golden and bubbly, 25 to 30 minutes. Serve immediately, sprinkled with the chives.

AUTUMN FEAST

HARVEST SOUP 158

FOIE GRAS TERRINE
WITH ARMAGNAC 168

CÈPE AND PARSLEY
TARTLETS 161

QUAIL GRILLED OVER
GRAPEVINES 172

APPLE TART WITH ORANGE
FLOWER WATER 213

Autumn is the richest season of
all, with endless offerings and
countless ways to cook them.
We love to have one last big feast
outdoors, bathe in the warm
October winds, and eat anything and
everything we want—flavors of the
forest mixed with the bounty of
the harvest. A time of plenty.

CHOCOLATE MERINGUE SWIRLS *with* CHOCOLATE SAUCE *and* CRÈME CHANTILLY

Meringues are my absolute favorite dessert, fun to make and a joy to eat. I'm even prepared to go out on a limb and declare that I've gotten very good at making them. I've gained what I would call meringue confidence. I like my meringues to be slightly soft in the middle, which is the Italian way, and when I eat them, I like to close my eyes and imagine myself wearing a flowery dress and sitting on the stone steps of a beautiful old Italian church.

When I first made these meringues, I wasn't going to add any more goodies. But then my sweet tooth and penchant for cream got the better of me, and so while these are good enough on their own, a dollop of cream and a thick chocolate sauce render them simply divine. It's best to avoid making meringues on rainy days, as the humidity may leave them limp and unattractive.

PREHEAT THE OVEN to 275°F/135°C. Line a baking sheet with parchment paper.

Using an electric mixer, whip the egg whites in a very clean bowl (make sure the bowl is free of any trace of oil) until they hold medium peaks. Add the salt and whip, adding the cornstarch and then the sugar 2 tablespoons at a time, until all of the sugar has been added, then continue to whip until the whites are stiff and glossy, 10 to 15 minutes total. Gently fold in the cocoa powder.

You want to make 6 meringues, each about 4 to 5 inches/10 to 12 cm wide and 2.5 inches/6 cm high, and you want to create nice swirls with the

(recipe continues)

6 large egg whites, at room temperature

A pinch of fine sea salt

1 tablespoon cornstarch

1⅔ cup/330 g granulated sugar

2 tablespoons unsweetened cocoa powder, plus more for dusting

¾ cup/180 ml heavy cream

Chocolate Sauce (recipe follows)

whites. With the help of two large spoons, spoon the egg whites onto the baking sheet; twirl one of the spoons around and finish off each meringue with a spiky peak. Dust some cocoa powder on top of each meringue and use a small fork to gently make a few more swirls.

Bake for 1 hour. Switch off the oven and leave the meringues in it, with the door slightly open, for 15 minutes. Remove from the oven and cool completely on a wire rack. The meringues are best served the same day.

To serve the meringues, whip the heavy cream until it holds stiff peaks. Put the meringues on serving plates, scoop some whipped cream next to each one, and drizzle with the chocolate sauce.

CHOCOLATE SAUCE

MIX THE WATER, cocoa powder, sugar, and Golden Syrup together in a small saucepan and bring to a low boil.

Remove from the heat, add the bittersweet chocolate, and stir gently until smooth. Let cool for an hour before serving.

MAKES ²/₃ CUP/ 160 ML

6½ tablespoons / 100 ml water

½ cup / 60 g unsweetened cocoa powder

¼ cup / 50 g granulated sugar

3 tablespoons Lyle's Golden Syrup or dark corn syrup

1 ounce / 30 g bittersweet chocolate, broken into small pieces

TOULOUSAINE VIOLET MERINGUES

At the end of a meal, I enjoy serving a selection of *mignardises*, small sweet confections that are sure to put a smile on my guests' faces. These little meringues, perfumed with violet essence, are timeless and close to my heart. Violets are emblematic of Toulouse and, by extension, nearby Moissac, where my mother's side of the family comes from. I can't tell you how many violet charms I collected as a girl! *La violette de Toulouse* is a Parma violet, sweet, fragrant, and luxurious. These tiny reproductions remind me of the original.

PREHEAT THE OVEN to 200°F/90°C. Line 2 baking sheets with parchment paper.

Using an electric mixer, whip the egg whites in a very clean bowl (make sure the bowl is free of any trace of oil) until they hold medium peaks. Add the salt and lemon juice and whip, adding the sugar 2 tablespoons at a time, until all of the sugar has been added, then whip until the whites are stiff and glossy, 10 to 15 minutes total. Add the violet extract and the food coloring, mixing until you have a pretty pastel purple color.

Gently spoon the meringue into a pastry bag fitted with a large star tip and pipe rosettes of meringue onto the baking sheet, leaving space between them; each one should be about 2 inches/5 cm wide.

Bake for 1 hour. Lower the oven temperature to 170°F/80°C and bake for 45 minutes.

Switch the oven off and let the meringues cool completely in the oven. The meringues can be kept in an airtight tin for up to 2 weeks. Serve with candied violets, if desired.

MAKES ABOUT 50 SMALL MERINGUES

2 large egg whites

Pinch of fine sea salt

½ teaspoon fresh lemon juice

⅔ cup/130 g granulated sugar

3 to 4 drops violet extract (found in specialty grocery stores), to taste

A few drops each of red and blue food coloring

Violet candies or candied violets (optional)

CALVADOS *and* CRÈME FRAÎCHE APPLE TART

When I think of my favorite desserts, it seems to me that a lot of them come from Normandy and Brittany, two regions famous for cream and butter, apples, and cider. A great dessert doesn't need to be overly sugary or sweet, too dressed up or fancy: sometimes just the right amount of flour, eggs, and butter (lots of it), mixed together in a certain way, can lead to magical things. The town of Calvados in Normandy is famous for its apple brandy (they also have a town called Camembert; you may have heard of it), and I always have a bottle at home. It's great as an after-dinner drink and works wonders in this recipe.

This rustic dessert is my ticket to Normandy, conjuring up its traditional houses with straw rooftops, windy beaches, black-and-white cows, and apple trees. They say that Normandy has the worst weather in France, but for me it's truly a beautiful place, one I am just as fond of as the south.

MAKE THE DOUGH. In a large bowl, mix together the flour, almond flour, confectioners' sugar, superfine sugar, salt, butter, and egg, stirring with a wooden spoon until the mixture forms a homogenous dough. Shape into a ball, flatten slightly, and wrap in plastic wrap. Refrigerate for at least 2 hours, or overnight.

Start the filling. Soak the apples in the Calvados in a medium bowl, stirring occasionally, for 1 hour.

Meanwhile, 30 minutes before rolling it out, remove the dough from the refrigerator.

SERVES 8

For the dough

2 cups / 240 g all-purpose flour, plus more for rolling

⅔ cup / 80 g almond flour

½ cup / 60 g confectioners' sugar

3 tablespoons superfine sugar

Pinch of fine sea salt

14 tablespoons / 1¾ sticks / 150 g unsalted butter, at room temperature

1 large egg

For the filling

5 medium apples (such as Empire, Gala, or Cortland), peeled, cored, and cut into small chunks

¼ cup / 60 ml Calvados

5 tablespoons / 60 g dark brown sugar

1 cup / 250 ml crème fraîche or sour cream

3 large egg yolks

3 tablespoons almond flour

Crème fraîche or sour cream for serving (optional)

On a floured parchment-covered surface, roll the dough into a 13-inch/ 33 cm circle ¼ inch/0.5 mm thick. Line an 11-inch/27-cm tart pan with the dough, fitting it into the base and up the sides. Trim the excess dough, leaving a ¼-inch/1-cm overhang. Fold over the excess dough to reinforce the edge. Pierce the dough all over with a fork. Freeze for 30 minutes to 1 hour to prevent shrinkage during baking.

Preheat the oven to 350°F/180°C.

Line the tart shell with parchment paper and fill with pie weights or dried beans. Bake for 10 minutes. Remove the parchment and weights, return the tart shell to the oven, and bake until the bottom is dry, about 6 minutes. Remove from the oven.

Drain the apples, reserving the Calvados. Sprinkle the base of the tart shell with 2 tablespoons/25 g of the brown sugar and spoon the apples into it.

Bake until the apples are slightly golden, about 30 minutes. If the crust starts to brown too much, cover the edges with aluminum foil. Remove from the oven.

In a small bowl, beat together the reserved Calvados, the remaining 3 tablespoons/35 g brown sugar, the crème fraîche, and egg yolks. Pour the mixture over the apples. Sprinkle the almond flour on top and bake until the custard is just set, about an additional 15 minutes; do not overbake. Remove from the oven and let cool for 10 minutes.

Serve the tart warm with crème fraîche on the side, if desired.

NOTE: *The tart is best served warm. As it cools, the filling settles and falls a little.*

APPLE TART *with*
ORANGE FLOWER WATER

One ingredient I can't live without is orange flower water. My earliest memory of *fleur d'oranger* dates back to when I was four or five, in Moissac. I don't know if I discovered it in pancakes or if it was in my grandmother's cologne. What I do remember for sure was a packet of *merveilles*, little fritters, sold by an elderly woman in the corner of the square. They were so good, on the crunchy side, and perfumed with the delicate scent of orange blossoms. I put orange flower water in madeleines, waffles, desserts—wherever I can (I even dab some behind my children's ears sometimes)—because the scent brings me back to my childhood.

MAKE THE DOUGH. Mix together the flour, sugar, and salt in a large bowl. Use your fingertips to rub in the butter until the mixture resembles fine crumbs. Mix in just enough cold water to make a smooth, pliable dough. Shape into a ball, flatten slightly, and wrap in plastic wrap. Refrigerate for at least 1 hour, or overnight.

Peel, core, and dice 2 of the apples. In a small saucepan, combine the diced apples, 3 tablespoons of the muscovado sugar, and the orange flower water and cook over low heat until the apples are soft, 10 to 15 minutes.

Purée the apple mixture with a potato masher until smooth. Set the compote aside to cool.

On a lightly floured work surface, roll out the dough into a 12-inch/30-cm circle ¼ inch/0.5 mm thick. Fit into the base and up the sides of a 10-inch/25-cm tart pan. Trim off any excess dough. Prick the base all over

(recipe continues)

For the dough

1⅔ cups/200 g all-purpose flour, sifted, plus more for rolling

1 tablespoon granulated sugar

Pinch of fine sea salt

8 tablespoons/1 stick/ 120 g unsalted butter, cut into cubes, at room temperature

1 to 2 tablespoons ice-cold water

For the filling

5 large apples

¼ cup/45 g muscovado sugar or other raw brown sugar

2 tablespoons orange flower water

with a fork. Cover with plastic wrap and freeze for 30 minutes to prevent shrinkage during baking.

Preheat the oven to 400°F/200°C.

Spread the apple compote evenly over the base of the tart shell. Peel, core, and thinly slice the remaining 3 apples. Arrange the apples in concentric circles on top of the compote, slightly overlapping the slices. Sprinkle with the remaining tablespoon of muscovado sugar.

Bake until the pastry is golden and the apples are nicely browned, about 30 minutes. Let cool on a wire rack for at least 15 minutes before serving.

Serve the tart warm or at room temperature.

BUTTER

We all have our mortal fears: mine is running out of butter. The refrigerator is a bank of sorts, and I don't feel relaxed unless I have at least two packs of unsalted butter in my savings account. Plus one salty one. Even then I am fidgety—I need more security. More than for cooking, though, I think this has to do with baking. Just the thought of being able, without advance notice or preparation, to bake a cake puts me at ease. The butter in my refrigerator and the eggs in my pantry are part of my investment in future good meals.

GALETTE PÉROUGIENNE

This is a wonderful specialty from the medieval town of Pérouges, near Lyon, made from a lemony yeasted brioche dough that is sprinkled with a generous amount of sugar, dotted with butter, and baked in a very hot oven. The sugar caramelizes and each bite is a pure delight. I am very fond of this medieval cake. It is so authentic and simple in taste—exactly what I look for in a dessert.

MIX THE YEAST in the lukewarm water in a small cup. Set aside for 5 minutes to allow the yeast to dissolve.

In a large bowl, mix together 8 tablespoons/120 g of the butter with the egg, lemon zest, salt, and 2 tablespoons of the sugar. Add the yeast mixture and then gradually add the flour, mixing with a wooden spoon until you have a soft and elastic dough.

Shape the dough into a ball, put it in a buttered bowl, cover with a damp cloth, and let rise in a warm spot until doubled in size, at least 2 hours.

Preheat the oven 450°F/230°C. Line a baking sheet with parchment paper.

On a parchment-paper-lined surface, roll the dough into a 9-inch/23-cm circle about ½ inch/1 cm thick. Press on the edges to make a ½-inch/1-cm-wide raised border. Sprinkle the remaining 6 tablespoons/75 g sugar over the dough and dot with the remaining 4 tablespoons/60 g butter.

Transfer to the baking sheet and bake until golden and caramelized, 15 minutes. Let cool for 5 minutes and serve warm.

SERVES 4 TO 6

2 teaspoons active dry yeast

⅓ cup/80 ml lukewarm water

12 tablespoons/ 1½ sticks/180 g unsalted butter, plus more for the bowl, at room temperature

1 large egg

Grated zest of 1 lemon

Pinch of fine sea salt

½ cup/100 g granulated sugar

1⅓ cups/160 g all-purpose flour, sifted, plus more for rolling

WINTER

We arrived in Médoc in late October, when the vineyards were golden and plucked and the weather was wet. There was silent beauty all around, but we couldn't escape the feeling that had we come a few weeks earlier, we could have enjoyed some al fresco dinners, a few dips in the pool. People spoke of the cèpes that were now gone and glorious harvest feasts just weeks ago. Our neighbors were preparing for winter, gathering wood and pinecones, making jam. But we weren't ready to hibernate. We wanted to explore the region, make discoveries. We quickly found the best markets and some nice restaurants that hadn't yet closed down for the winter. We took long walks with the dogs on the endless stretches of unspoiled beaches and dreamt of future summer days with picnic baskets and chilled rosé.

The huge rosemary bush just outside the kitchen was a source of inspiration for my cooking those first few weeks; there was a lot of lamb on our table that month. In November, we found a bay tree with the most aromatic leaves just outside our garden gate. Nature might be dormant—the apples gone, the leaves falling—but we could still make use of some of her riches. By December, we felt pretty familiar with the region. We had fun visiting châteaus and buying wine; we even found the best baguette in Médoc (we haven't changed our minds on that one). We had oysters twice a week and my husband stopped cutting himself when he opened them. We stopped locking our door; the gunshots and insistent barking of the hunting groups that passed by our house didn't startle me any longer. We had frequent visits from all sorts of creatures of the forest: hares, wild boars, deer, frogs, and snakes are regulars, although the smart ones quickly discovered that a house with fourteen dogs is not the place to be. We began to feel a little bit like real Médocains, but in truth, we had barely scratched the surface.

That first year, a few days before Christmas, two of our puppies went missing after chasing a flock of deer. We scoured the area, called the local authorities, and alerted neighbors, but by nightfall they still weren't home. Just five months old and lost in the forest, amongst foxes and worse. I couldn't sleep at all that night and we spent hours shouting their names into the woods, like wolves howling for their babies. The next few days were spent combing the area, widening the circle of search, calling people. We drove down every road and path we could find in our city car, and we got stuck and saved over and over. Some of the narrow country roads led to dilapidated houses. There would be smoke coming from the chimney, chickens and ducks and dogs and sometimes donkeys milling about outside. Usually a man

with very few teeth would come out and greet us, and often we could see his wife in the doorway peeking at us, a big pot of something brewing on the stove. None of them had seen our dogs, and weren't even familiar with fox terriers. "Are they hunting dogs?" the men would ask. I got so worried they would keep the little puppies for themselves if they found them that we started saying they were utterly useless. It was all very Hansel and Gretel. Dark thoughts crept in, like, *Maybe this isn't a place for us after all.*

The day before Christmas, we got a call from the *mairie* (town hall); a man had found two dogs that he believed were ours. Could he come and see us, and did we have a little something for him? Indeed they were our dogs, and in good shape, too. The man, looking a bit sheepish, said he'd taken good care of the puppies, that he had toyed with the idea of keeping them but then thought, *It's almost Christmas, they are so cute, someone must miss them.* We thanked him, gave him that little something, and said our good-byes. As he was walking to his car, he turned and said mischievously, "Why did you leave Paris for Médoc? Nothing ever happens here." He didn't wait for an answer and continued, "The people are a bit boring, don't you think? All they talk about is mushrooms and oysters and wine and the weather." "Those are my favorite topics," I replied. He smiled and then he was gone. From that moment, I knew I would stay here for a long time.

Now we've been here a few years and while I still prefer summer, the rural French winter is starting to agree with me. There is something strangely comforting about Sunday mornings when the stone floors of the house are ice cold and I not only feel the chill but can actually see it through my bedroom window as I lie in bed. Staring out at the bare branches, admiring the lifeless beauty, is a privilege of country life. Then a dog inevitably jumps into the picture. My husband always wakes up early because of the dogs and sometimes brings me tea in bed, which is most appreciated. If I am feeling courageous, I sometimes dress warmly and cycle to the village to get provisions. I fill the basket on my bike with a piece of meat, a fresh baguette, and lots of vegetables. Riding home, through peaceful and often icy pastures, brings me serenity and my mind wanders from the sights around me to the food I will be cooking. On days like that, bringing home the groceries feels like an achievement.

In winter, my kitchen table still life includes beets and turnips and pumpkins and nuts and . . . just looking at the table with its palette of choices—beautiful produce waiting to be turned

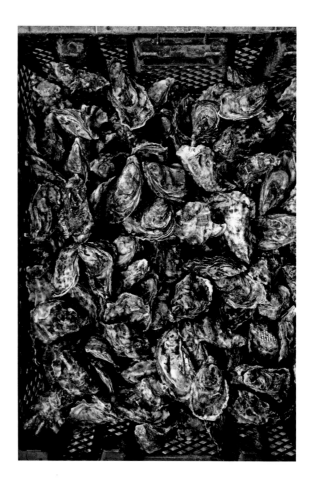

into something even more wonderful—inspires me to cook. I take great pride in arranging the vegetables and fruits, as if they were going to be painted or photographed (the latter actually quite likely, given Oddur's inclinations). During those cold days, my cooking takes a bourgeois turn and I prepare slow-cooked meals that simmer forever on the stove and fill the house with warmth and wonderful aromas. Some dishes just can't be enjoyed properly in warm weather—and they are my favorite thing about winter.

STARTERS

Eggs en Cocotte with Mushrooms

Potato Pie with Comté Cheese

Vol-au-Vent

Roquefort and Walnut Gougères

Winter Vegetable Cocotte

Garlic Soup

L'Ami Jean's Parmesan Soup

Chestnut Velouté

MAIN COURSES
AND A SIDE

Coq au Vin

Garbure des Pyrénées

Roast Guinea Hen with Herbs

Roasted Sausages with Red Wine and Fennel

Beef Cheek Stew

Oxtail Macaroni Gratin

Blanquette de Veau

Roast Potatoes with Herbs and Garlic (side dish)

DESSERTS

Pear Flognarde

Sarah Bernhardt Cakes

Kouign Amann

Salted-Butter Crème Caramel

Mont Blanc

Chestnut Ice Cream

Madeleines with Pistachio Pots de Crème

Old-Fashioned Waffles

CHINESE NEW YEAR

EGGS EN COCOTTE
with MUSHROOMS

I was once asked what my favorite ingredient to cook with is. After giving it some thought, I decided it must be eggs—so humble yet rich, and endlessly versatile. Give me a dozen eggs and a few other basics, and I'll be fine. Here in Bordeaux, they like to cook them in wine (of course) with shallots (of course) and it makes for a delicious little treat. My version includes chanterelles and broth and I favor spring onions instead of shallots. I always serve them with *mouillettes*, toasted sliced baguette, slightly rubbed with garlic to give that extra flavor when you dip them in the runny eggs. In our family, we often have this for dinner when lunch has dragged on almost until evening and we just need a little something to tide us over until morning. It makes a pleasant start to any meal, and it is equally welcome when served at midnight after an evening at the theatre.

PREHEAT THE OVEN to 400°F/ 200°C.

In a small saucepan, heat the olive oil over medium heat. Add the onion and cook until softened, 3 to 4 minutes. Add the wine and simmer to reduce for 2 minutes. Add the stock, 2 teaspoons of the butter, and salt and pepper. Reduce the heat to low and cook until the sauce is slightly thickened and glossy, 4 to 5 minutes.

Meanwhile, prepare the mushrooms. In a large sauté pan, heat the remaining tablespoon of butter over high heat. Cook the mushrooms for 2 minutes. Add the minced garlic and the parsley, season with salt and pepper, and cook until the mushrooms are slightly soft, 1 minute more.

(recipe continues)

SERVES 4

1 tablespoon extra-virgin olive oil

1 spring onion, thinly sliced

Scant ½ cup/100 ml dry red wine

Scant ½ cup/100 ml chicken or vegetable stock

1 tablespoon plus 2 teaspoons unsalted butter

Fine sea salt and freshly ground black pepper

5 ounces/150 g chanterelle mushrooms

1 garlic clove, cut in half, one half minced

2 tablespoons finely chopped fresh parsley

4 large eggs

Rub the inside of four individual ramekins with the halved garlic clove and spoon the mushrooms into them. Crack the eggs into the ramekins. Pour some sauce over each egg and season with salt and pepper. (You can also make this in one 6-inch/14-cm baking dish.)

Put the ramekins in a baking dish and pour enough boiling water into the dish to come halfway up the sides of the ramekins. Bake until the whites are set but the yolks are still runny, 12 to 15 minutes.

Serve immediately.

POTATO PIE *with* COMTÉ CHEESE

I am constantly making savory pies and tarts, often with meat in them, but they can be just as delicious made with potatoes—and a little cheese. My mother would sometimes take me to a tea salon in Paris where we'd share a potato pie after a shopping session. One day, I had a yearning for that pie from my childhood, so I made it from memory. I don't think the original had Comté cheese in it, but since that is my all-time favorite cheese, I couldn't resist. This pie can easily be served as a meal on its own, but served as a starter, it adds a decadent (and very filling) touch to an elaborate Sunday lunch. It can be prepared in advance, travels very well, and so is ideal to take to other people's houses. I am a big fan of Bordeaux wines, but this pie is most perfectly paired with a slightly chilled red Burgundy.

IN A MEDIUM SAUTÉ PAN, heat 1 teaspoon of the olive oil and cook the bacon until crisp, about 4 minutes. Using a slotted spoon, transfer to a plate.

Heat the remaining teaspoon of olive oil in the same pan, and cook the onion for 3 minutes. Add the garlic and cook until the onion is golden, about 2 minutes more. Season with salt and pepper. Set aside to cool for 5 minutes.

Preheat the oven to 400°F/200°C.

Divide the dough in half. On a lightly floured work surface, roll out each piece of dough ¼ inch/0.5 cm thick. You want a slightly larger base (about 12 inches/30 cm in diameter) and a slightly smaller top layer (about 9 inches/23 cm in diameter).

(recipe continues)

2 teaspoons extra-virgin olive oil

4 ounces / 120 g bacon, cut crosswise into ¼-inch / 6.3-mm-wide strips (lardons)

2 onions, thinly sliced

3 garlic cloves, thinly sliced

All-purpose flour for rolling

Double recipe of Tart Dough (page 79)

2 pounds / 900 g russet potatoes, peeled and sliced into thin rounds

Fine sea salt and freshly ground black pepper

2 cups / 190 g diced Comté cheese

½ teaspoon grated nutmeg

½ teaspoon fresh thyme leaves

2 tablespoons / 30 g unsalted butter, cut into small pieces

1 large egg yolk

1 tablespoon heavy cream

Line a 9½-inch/24-cm pie dish with one circle of dough, leaving ¾-inch/ 2-cm overhang. Add a layer of half of the potatoes, season with salt and pepper, and follow with layers of the onions, bacon, and cheese. Sprinkle with the nutmeg and thyme, scatter the bits of the butter on top, and finish with a layer of the remaining potatoes. Season with salt and pepper.

To make an egg wash, whisk the egg yolk with the cream. Brush the edges of the dough with the egg wash. Cover with the second circle of dough and seal by pressing firmly on the rim of the dish with your thumbs. Cut off the excess dough, reroll it, and cut out 5 to 7 leaves to decorate the pie. Press the leaves gently onto the dough. With the back of your knife, press lightly all around the edges of the pie to make a border. Pierce a hole in the center of the pie (I use a chopstick) to make a steam vent. Brush the pie with the remaining egg wash.

Bake the pie until golden brown, 40 to 45 minutes. Cover with parchment paper or foil if the pie browns too much. Serve warm or at room temperature.

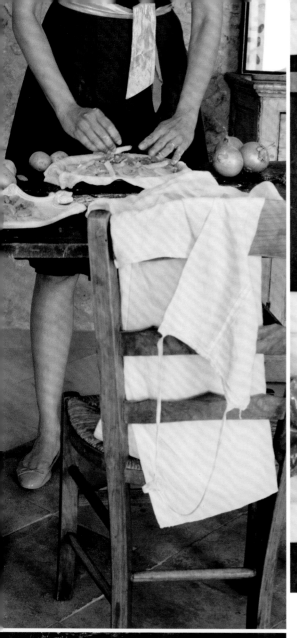

FRESH HERBS

I am a master of impromptu dinners, mostly because I am also a master of poor planning. I've been saved from embarrassment more times than I can remember by fresh herbs. Not everyone can have a bay tree or a huge rosemary bush, but any enthusiastic cook should make a point of growing her own herbs. They are often readily available in stores, but somehow the ones you need most are always the ones sold out: it's frustrating to have ten packs of mint in front of you when all you need is tarragon. And they are expensive, too. So I grow them all, boxes of them, in the windows, where I hang the laundry outdoors, and outside the guest bedroom. We have tarragon for omelettes, sage for pork chops and butter sauces, and an abundance of thyme for everything. It may be a contradiction in terms, but I say, if you only grow one thing, grow lots of different herbs.

VOL·AU·VENT

VOL·AU·VENT

When I make this, I think of ladies who lunch. Perhaps it's the grandeur of the presentation or even the cute little hat that looks so chic. Whatever it is, I still haven't met a woman who doesn't go a little crazy for a well-made vol-au-vent. I used to have this dish occasionally at Ladurée in Paris, where it's served at its most classic, with sweetbreads and morel mushrooms, and only in winter—and that's how I like it. But for me, a vol-au-vent is an idea more than a recipe. You take some puff pastry and make a little nest out of it. Then you fill it with a creamy sauce flush with mushrooms and meat, and voilà. If you do not want to use sweetbreads, simply omit them. Even the name of the pastry is open for interpretation—something like "blown by the wind" or "up in the air" might do. I like to call it "gone with the wind." And I always make more than I need, because someone always wants seconds.

PUT THE SWEETBREADS in a bowl and cover with water mixed with 1 tablespoon of the coarse salt. Refrigerate overnight.

Preheat the oven to 400°F/200°C. Line a baking sheet with parchment paper.

If using puff pastry, on a lightly floured surface, roll out the dough ¼ inch/0.5 mm thick. With a 3-inch/7-cm round pastry cutter, cut out 20 disks. Gently mark half of the pastry circles with a smaller pastry cutter, 2 inches/5 cm in diameter, so that once the pastry is baked, you can easily cut out the center part and scoop in the filling. Brush a little beaten egg on the base rings (the unmarked ones), then place the marked rings on top and brush again with the egg. Transfer to the lined baking sheet.

1 pound / 450 g veal sweetbreads

2 tablespoons coarse sea salt

1 tablespoon all-purpose flour, plus more for rolling

1 pound / 450 g puff pastry, homemade (page 28) or store-bought, defrosted if frozen, or ten 3-inch / 7-cm ready-made puff pastry cases

1 large egg, lightly beaten

1 bay leaf

2 cloves

10 tablespoons / 1¼ sticks / 150 g unsalted butter

2 shallots, thinly sliced

12 ounces / 350 g boneless, skinless chicken breasts, sliced into strips

Fine sea salt and freshly ground black pepper

Leaves from a few sprigs of fresh thyme

¼ teaspoon grated nutmeg

Juice of ½ lemon

Bake the pastry cases until well risen and golden, 10 to 12 minutes. Let cool on wire racks for 5 minutes. With the tip of a sharp knife, cut out the 2-inch caps and set aside. Dig out a bit of pastry to make room for the filling. Let cool completely.

Drain the sweetbreads. Pull off and discard the outer membranes and veins. Transfer the sweetbreads to a large pot. Cover with water, add the remaining tablespoon of coarse salt, the bay leaf, and cloves and bring to a boil. Remove from the heat and let stand for 15 minutes. Drain the sweetbreads and cut into small cubes.

In a large sauté pan, heat 5 tablespoons/75 g of the butter over medium heat. Cook the shallots until softened, 5 minutes. Add the sweetbreads and chicken, season with salt and pepper, and sprinkle in the 1 tablespoon of flour, the thyme leaves, and nutmeg. Cook until the meat is opaque, 5 minutes. Add the lemon juice and simmer for 3 minutes. Add 1 tablespoon of the Armagnac and simmer for 2 minutes. Remove the chicken to a plate and keep warm; leave the sweetbreads in the pan. Reduce the heat to low, cover, and cook until the sweetbreads are cooked through, 15 minutes.

Meanwhile, in another large sauté pan, heat the remaining 5 tablespoons/75 g butter over medium heat. Cook the mushrooms until softened, 5 minutes. Season with salt and pepper. Lower the heat and stir in the crème fraîche, then remove from the heat.

Add the chicken, the remaining 1 tablespoon Armagnac, and the morel cream sauce to the cooked sweetbreads and gently mix together with a wooden spoon. Cook gently over low heat for a few seconds just to combine the flavors. Check the seasoning.

Spoon the mixture into the pastry cases. Sprinkle with the parsley, put the caps back on top, and serve immediately.

2 tablespoons Armagnac

12 ounces/350 g morel or other mushrooms, preferably seasonal and wild

1 cup/250 ml crème fraîche

A handful of finely chopped fresh parsley

ROQUEFORT
and WALNUT GOUGÈRES

In France, we'll take any excuse to open a bottle of bubbly—whether it's Bastille Day or your dog's birthday! So the question arises, what to serve with all that Champagne? Gougères are airy little cheese puffs so seductive that guests will find it impossible to stop eating them. I make them extra glamorous with Roquefort and walnuts. The trick is finding the right balance of how many to serve: too many, and your guests will lose their appetite for the dinner you've been cooking all day; too few, and they will feel cheated. I think two to three per person is just about right, or maybe four or five or . . .

PREHEAT THE OVEN to 350°F/180°C. Line a baking sheet with parchment paper.

In a medium saucepan, bring the water and butter to a boil. Add the flour, stirring very fast with a wooden spoon, then take off the heat and mix until the dough is smooth. Return to the heat and cook, stirring constantly, for 1 minute to dry the dough slightly. By now, the dough will be roughly in the form of a soft ball. Remove from the heat and add the eggs one at a time. Add the Roquefort, nutmeg, and half of the walnuts, season with salt and pepper, and stir well.

You have two choices for forming the gougères: Put the dough in a pastry bag with a plain medium tip and pipe walnut-sized mounds or shape them into balls with the help of two teaspoons. Leave adequate space between the gougères. Glaze with the egg yolk and sprinkle with the remaining walnuts.

Bake the gougères until puffed and golden, about 25 minutes. Serve immediately.

MAKES ABOUT 40 GOUGÈRES

1 cup/240 ml water

7 tablespoons/100 g unsalted butter

1¼ cups/150 g all-purpose flour

4 large eggs

3½ ounces/100 g Roquefort cheese, crumbled

Pinch of grated nutmeg

⅓ cup plus 1 tablespoon/60 g walnuts, coarsely chopped

Fine sea salt and freshly ground black pepper

1 large egg yolk, lightly beaten

NOTE: *You can prepare these in advance and freeze them. After baking, let them cool completely on a wire rack. Put them in an air-tight container, placing parchment paper between the layers, and cover with the lid. They can be stored in the freezer for up to 2 months.*

WINTER VEGETABLE COCOTTE

I love using *cocottes*, or cast-iron Dutch ovens, when I cook. They have a certain rustic allure to them and make every dish seem more bistro-like and tasty. I have several big ones and plenty of little ones that can be used for individual servings. Putting a piping-hot cocotte on the dining table and ceremonially lifting off the lid with a thick cloth always gets everybody's attention. Usually they can't wait for me to unveil what's inside and let the aromas perfume the air. In winter, I like to flavor colorful vegetable stews with a well-chosen piece of slab bacon. This is not a rigid recipe; any of the vegetables can be replaced by other seasonal ones as you wish. Additionally, it can also be served as a starter, or side, as well as a main dish.

IN A MEDIUM COCOTTE or other heavy pot, heat the olive oil over medium heat. Cook the onion until tender, about 3 minutes. Add the bacon and cook until lightly golden, 4 to 5 minutes.

Add the pumpkin, carrots, parsnip, celery, Jerusalem artichokes, chestnuts, and garlic, season with salt and pepper, and stir to combine. Cook for 5 minutes, then add the red wine and simmer to reduce for 2 minutes. Add the chicken stock, cover, and reduce the heat to low. Cook until the vegetables are tender but not mushy or overcooked, 20 to 25 minutes.

Stir in the butter, chives, and parsley and serve.

NOTE: *If you are using smoked slab bacon* (poitrine fumée), *I would suggest blanching it in boiling water for a few minutes before using to remove some of the saltiness.*

SERVES 4

2 tablespoons extra-virgin olive oil

1 onion, thinly sliced

5 ounces / 150 g slab bacon (see Note), diced

1 mini pumpkin (about 1½ pounds / 680 g), peeled, seeded, and cut into small chunks

2 carrots, peeled and diced

1 parsnip, peeled and diced

1 celery stalk, sliced

4 small Jerusalem artichokes, thinly sliced

15 peeled cooked chestnuts (jarred or vacuum-packed)

1 garlic clove, thinly sliced

Fine sea salt and freshly ground black pepper

3 tablespoons dry red wine

⅓ cup / 80 ml chicken or vegetable stock

1 tablespoon unsalted butter

A small handful of chopped fresh chives

A small handful of chopped fresh parsley

GARLIC SOUP

I don't feel right if there is not a mountain of garlic on my kitchen table ready to be mixed with butter, oil, or herbs; waiting to be caramelized, roasted, or eased into a sauce. *Comfort* may be an overused word, but if ever there were a comforting soup, it is this garlic one. There are moments in winter when my body (or my children) calls for it. I feel it protects me from illness just as it has protected generations of French farmers before me.

IN A LARGE POT, heat the duck fat over medium heat. Cook the onion for 2 minutes. Add the sliced head of garlic and cook until softened but not browned, about 2 minutes. Add the flour and stir well, then pour in the chicken stock and bring to a low boil. Season with salt and pepper, add the thyme sprigs, lower the heat, cover, and let simmer for 20 minutes.

Meanwhile, in a small sauté pan, heat the olive oil over medium heat. Fry the remaining sliced garlic until golden and slightly crisp, about 3 minutes. Drain on a paper towel.

Purée the soup in batches in a blender. Return the soup to the pot and set over medium heat.

Beat the egg whites in a small bowl and then drizzle, whisking constantly, into the soup. You should see thin strands of egg white form in the soup; immediately remove from the heat. Whisk the egg yolks with the vinegar in a small bowl, then slowly add a little of the soup, whisking constantly. Add the egg yolk mixture to the soup, again whisking constantly to prevent curdling.

Ladle the soup into bowls, sprinkle with the fried garlic, and drizzle with a few drops of olive oil, if desired. Serve immediately.

SERVES 4

2 tablespoons duck fat or extra-virgin olive oil

1 onion, finely diced

1 whole head garlic, plus 2 garlic cloves, thinly sliced

1 tablespoon all-purpose flour

5 cups / 1.2 liters chicken stock

Fine sea salt and freshly ground black pepper

A few sprigs of fresh thyme

1 tablespoon extra-virgin olive oil, plus, if desired, more for serving

2 large eggs, separated

1 tablespoon sherry vinegar

L'AMI JEAN'S PARMESAN SOUP

There are so many excellent restaurants in Paris that it's hard, and perhaps even pointless, to pick favorites. If I had to, though, Stéphane Jégo's L'Ami Jean would get my vote any day. I've been to the restaurant countless times and have never been disappointed. His cooking strikes the most elusive balance between traditional and inventive and strangely feels like home cooking while at the same time it feels special. One of the classics at his restaurant is this Parmesan soup, for which he generously lent me the recipe. It's been such a crowd-pleaser at my table for years that I just had to include it in this book. *Merci*, Stéphane!

SERVES 8 TO 10

4 tablespoons / 60 g unsalted butter

2 onions, coarsely chopped

7 ounces / 200 g Parmesan cheese, sliced

4 cups / 1 liter chicken stock

2 quarts / 2 liters heavy cream

4 cups / 1 liter whole milk

2 ounces / 50 g bacon, finely chopped

Fine sea salt and freshly ground black pepper

2 tablespoons croûtons (see page 107)

1 shallot, finely chopped

A handful of finely chopped fresh chives

MELT THE BUTTER in a large pot over low heat. Cook the onions until soft, 10 minutes. Add three-quarters of the Parmesan, the chicken stock, cream, and milk, bring to a simmer, and simmer until the ingredients are melted and the soup has thickened slightly, 45 minutes.

Meanwhile, in a small sauté pan, cook the bacon until crisp, about 5 minutes. Drain on a paper towel.

Add the remaining Parmesan to the soup and simmer for 10 minutes more.

Purée the soup in a blender in batches, then strain through a sieve. Season with salt and pepper.

Scatter the croutons, shallots, chives, and bacon into soup bowls, ladle the soup on top, and serve immediately.

CHESTNUT VELOUTÉ

I think everybody is attracted to certain specific flavors, ones that always appeal to them. I remember my father's finger going over menus in restaurants and always stopping at anything with braised pork. One of my key flavors is chestnuts. If I see the word *chataîgne* on a menu, I am sure to take a closer look. Chestnuts are one of the things I look forward to having when the days get shorter and the weather colder, and they very rarely let me down. My craving builds up slowly until Christmas, when it explodes and just about everything has chestnuts in it. Then we say a long good-bye until we meet again in the fall.

IN A LARGE POT, melt 2 tablespoons of the butter over medium heat. Cook the onion and leek until softened, about 5 minutes. Reserve 8 chestnuts and add the rest to the pot, along with the thyme and wine. Season with salt and pepper and cook for 5 minutes.

Pour the vegetable stock into the pot and bring to a boil. Reduce the heat and simmer for 30 minutes.

Meanwhile, coarsely chop the reserved chestnuts. In a small sauté pan, melt the remaining 1 tablespoon of butter over medium heat and cook the chestnuts until slightly golden, about 3 minutes.

Purée the soup in batches in a blender. Serve topped with the crème fraîche, chopped chestnuts, and chives.

SERVES 4

3 tablespoons unsalted butter

1 white onion, thinly sliced

1 leek, white part only, thinly sliced

2 pounds / 900 g peeled cooked chestnuts (jarred or vacuum-packed)

A few sprigs of fresh thyme

2 tablespoons dry white wine

Fine sea salt and freshly ground black pepper

6 cups / 1.5 liters vegetable stock

¼ cup / 60 ml crème fraîche

A few fresh chives, finely chopped

COQ AU VIN

There are so many versions of this national treasure of a dish. Some are overly elaborate, others simplified, most good in their own way. Purists, of course, will only make a *coq au vin* with an actual rooster, but we tend to use whatever bird we can get our hands on, usually a big high-quality chicken. I say "we" because my husband loves to make this dish at home. He wants the sauce to be thick, "inky," and studded with pearl onions; I find it necessary to add some cèpes. We agree that the chicken has to marinate overnight. Apparently *coq au vin* was the lunch my husband had right before we met in Paris many years ago. Perhaps it reminds him of his single days, but he says it reminds him of me because it was the prelude to our first encounter. I prefer that version.

MARINATE THE CHICKEN. In a large bowl, combine the chicken, onion, garlic, and wine. Season with salt and pepper. Cover with plastic wrap and refrigerate overnight, stirring once or twice during the process.

Meanwhile, prepare the stock. Heat the oil in a large heavy pot over high heat. Add the chicken back and wings and brown, stirring regularly to avoid burning, for about 5 minutes. Transfer to a plate. Add the onion, carrots, leek, celery and cook until golden brown, about 5 minutes. Return the chicken back and wings to the pot and pour in enough water to cover the chicken. Add the bouquet garni, peppercorns, and cloves and bring to a boil. Lower the heat and simmer, skimming impurities off the surface regularly, until reduced by half, about 2 hours. Let cool, then strain, discarding the solids, and refrigerate until needed, or overnight.

Remove the chicken pieces from the marinade and pat dry. Drain the onion and garlic, reserving the wine, and pat dry.

SERVES 6

For the chicken

1 large chicken
(4½ to 5½ pounds/
2 to 2.5 kg), cut into
8 pieces (reserve the
back and wings for
the stock)

1 large onion, coarsely
chopped

1 head garlic,
separated into
cloves, crushed, and
peeled

1 (750-ml) bottle
reasonably good
Bordeaux

Fine sea salt and
freshly ground black
pepper

7 ounces/200 g
smoked bacon, cut
crosswise into thin
strips

3 tablespoons unsalted
butter

1 tablespoon all-
purpose flour

¼ cup/60 ml Cognac

A handful of dried
or frozen cèpes
(porcini)

15 pearl onions

7 ounces/200 g small
white mushrooms

Bring a medium saucepan of water to a boil. Add the bacon and blanch for 3 minutes. Drain and pat dry.

Transfer the bacon to a Dutch oven or other pot (large enough to hold the chicken), add half of the butter, and cook until the bacon is golden, about 4 minutes. Remove the bacon with a slotted spoon and drain on paper towels.

Return the Dutch oven to medium heat. Season the chicken pieces with salt and pepper and brown in the fat remaining in the pot, turning once, about 8 minutes. When the chicken pieces are golden brown, remove from the pot and add the reserved vegetables in their place. Cook gently until translucent and golden, about 6 minutes.

Return the chicken pieces to the pot, add the bacon, sprinkle with the flour, and cook, stirring, for 2 minutes. Pour in the Cognac, light a match, and carefully ignite the liquid to flambé. When the flame has died out, pour in the wine and enough chicken stock to cover all the ingredients. Bring to a boil, then add the cèpes, reduce the heat, and simmer until the chicken is tender but not falling off the bones, about 1 hour or so, depending on the size of the pieces and the age of the bird (a mature rooster will take at least 2 hours).

Meanwhile, halfway through the cooking time, melt the remaining butter in a small sauté pan over medium heat. Add the pearl onions and sauté them for a few minutes, then add the white mushrooms. Season with salt and pepper and cook until the onions and mushrooms are golden, about 5 minutes, then add to the simmering chicken.

When the meat is tender, carefully transfer the pieces of chicken to a plate. Boil the sauce over high heat until reduced to the desired thickness, 8 to 10 minutes. Return the chicken to the pot and serve immediately.

For the chicken stock

2 tablespoons extra-virgin olive oil

1 onion, coarsely chopped

2 carrots, sliced

1 leek, white and pale green parts, chopped

2 celery stalks, chopped

1 bouquet garni (see page 159)

1 tablespoon black peppercorns

2 cloves

GARBURE DES PYRÉNÉES

Some encounters are more serendipitous than others. You might work with someone your whole life and never become very close, or you might meet someone once and the encounter has a lasting impact. It could be something that was said, a piece of advice, a shared experience. In my case, it was a recipe.

Bernard Vanderhooven is an antiques dealer I met by chance in Bordeaux. He is a real bon vivant and we got on like a house on fire. His recipe for *garbure*, a hearty soup studded with chopped vegetables and pork, is simply the most comforting food you can imagine having on a dark winter's night. When I make it, I sometimes think of Bernard coming into his lavishly decorated apartment after a long cold day at the antiques fair. I imagine him taking off his hat, greeting his cat, pouring himself a nice glass of Bordeaux, and enjoying a bowl of the soup he would have made the night before. I imagine he listens to jazz. Cheers, Bernard.

PUT THE BEANS in a medium bowl and add enough cold water to cover them by at least 2 inches/5 cm. Let soak overnight in a cool place. In a separate bowl, cover the ham hock with water and let soak overnight in the refrigerator.

The next day, heat the duck fat in a very large pot, over medium heat. Add the carrots, leeks, onions, garlic, and cabbage and cook until slightly softened, 3 to 4 minutes. Season with salt and pepper. Drain the ham hock and add to the pot, along with the pig's tail, if using. Cover with water and bring to a low boil, then cover, lower the heat, and simmer until the ham hock meat is very tender, about 3 hours.

SERVES 6 TO 8

2 cups / 360 g dried white beans

2 pounds / 1 kg smoked ham hock

¼ cup / 59 ml rendered duck fat, or extra-virgin olive oil or 4 tablespoons / 60 g unsalted butter

6 carrots, halved crosswise and cut into 1½-inch / 4-cm sticks

5 leeks, white and pale green parts, coarsely chopped

4 onions, quartered

5 garlic cloves, halved

1 medium Savoy cabbage, cut into 8 wedges

Fine sea salt and freshly ground black pepper

6 small to medium russet potatoes

1 pig's tail (optional)

Drain the beans and add to the pot, along with the potatoes. Simmer until the beans and potatoes are cooked and tender, about 1 hour longer.

Transfer the ham hock and pig's tail, if you have it, to a cutting board. Remove the meat, discarding the skin and bones. Shred the meat into the soup and serve.

ROAST GUINEA HEN *with* HERBS

Christmas, to me, means having some sort of bird. I have never gotten into turkey, but quail, squab, and ducks are all welcome visitors during the festivities. There is something so beautiful about a whole roasted bird (or birds) in the middle of the dining table, surrounded by candlelight, wine in crystal glasses, glistening silverware, and all sorts of side dishes. Through the years I've experimented with various ways of cooking guinea hen, and I've reached the conclusion that this great-tasting bird shouldn't be tampered with too much; a few herbs and some duck fat do the trick nicely. At Christmas we tend to have many courses and endless extras—it sometimes feels as if lunch and dinner overlap—so one large bird is usually enough for the family. It's always important to leave a bit of space for dessert, and at Christmas it's an absolute necessity.

One 3-pound / 1.5-kg guinea hen

¼ cup / 60 g duck fat or extra-virgin olive oil

Fine sea salt and freshly ground black pepper

3 garlic cloves, unpeeled

1 lemon, cut in quarters

A bunch of fresh thyme

A few sprigs of fresh rosemary

3 bay leaves

TAKE THE GUINEA HEN out of the refrigerator 30 minutes before cooking. Preheat the oven to 400°F / 200°C.

Rub the bird with the duck fat. Season generously both inside and out with salt and pepper. Put the garlic cloves, lemon, thyme, rosemary, and bay leaves in the cavity. Put the bird in a roasting pan.

Roast until golden and cooked through (the juices should run clear, not pink, when you prick the thigh with a knife), 40 to 50 minutes. Carve and serve.

NOTE: *If you'd like to serve this dish with potatoes, add 1 pound/900 g new potatoes, scrubbed and cut in half, to the roasting pan, scattering them around the guinea hen. Sprinkle with salt and drizzle with a bit of duck fat or olive oil.*

ROASTED SAUSAGES
with RED WINE *and* FENNEL

I have a very good relationship with my butcher and I am always open to his advice. One day, when I entered the shop he had an odd look on his face, as if he had been waiting for me. He certainly had something to tell me. "You have to try these," he said, holding up a strand of sausage links. "These look like ordinary chipolatas, but they are not; they are much better. I sourced them locally." I hadn't had any intention of buying sausages that day, but after such a presentation, I couldn't bear to let him down. I cooked them that night, roasting them with onion and fennel, finishing them with red wine. It was an immediate hit and has become one of the top ten dishes I cook most often because it's so tasty and easy. Serve with Garlic Mashed Potatoes (page 123).

PREHEAT THE OVEN to 350°F/180°C.

In a small bowl, mix together the olive oil and mustard. Put the sausages in a baking dish big enough to hold them snugly in one layer, drizzle with mustard mixture, and turn to coat.

Roast the sausages for 20 minutes.

Take the baking dish out of the oven, add the fennel, onion, and thyme, and season lightly with salt (the sausages are likely already salted) and pepper. Mix the ingredients together so they get coated in oil.

Return to the oven and roast until the sausages are cooked through and golden, about 25 minutes more, stirring halfway through the cooking.

Add the red wine and butter and roast until the wine has reduced and the sauce has become slightly thicker, about 10 minutes. Serve hot.

SERVES 4 TO 6

2 tablespoons extra-
  virgin olive oil

1 tablespoon Dijon
  mustard

12 good-quality pork
  sausages

1 large fennel bulb,
  trimmed and sliced

1 large onion, sliced

  A few sprigs of fresh
  thyme

  Coarse sea salt and
  freshly ground black
  pepper

1 cup/240 ml dry red
  wine

2 tablespoons unsalted
  butter

BEEF CHEEK STEW

I love stews that cook forever in wine, creating incredible flavors and aromas. These are the cozy dishes that make a cold winter enjoyable and warm. In spring, I am happy to take a break from them, but I often find myself yearning for a hearty stew as early as August. I will wake up in the morning with a beef cheek stew on my brain and say to my husband, "It's so cold this morning. I think we need to have something comforting today." He will try to explain to me that the weather forecast is predicting scorching temperatures later in the day, but by then I'm probably already in the kitchen chopping carrots.

The kids love to have this dish with little pasta coquillettes (macaroni shells); I like it with potatoes. To each his own.

PUT THE BEEF CHEEKS in a large bowl. Add the carrots, leek, shallots, garlic, bouquet garni, lemon zest, piment d'Espelette, and wine. Cover and refrigerate overnight.

Remove the beef from the marinade and pat dry. Drain the vegetables, reserving the wine. Season the beef with salt and pepper.

In a large Dutch oven, heat the oil and butter over medium heat. Brown the beef on all sides, about 5 minutes. Sprinkle in the flour and stir well. Add the reserved marinade ingredients except for the wine and cook for 3 minutes.

Pour the wine into the pot, add the tomatoes, and season with salt and pepper. Reduce the heat to low, cover, and simmer, adding a little water if the liquid reduces too much, until the meat is fork-tender, 2 to 3 hours.

Serve hot.

SERVES 6 TO 8

2½ pounds / 1.2 kg beef cheeks

6 carrots, peeled and coarsely chopped

1 leek, white and pale green parts, finely chopped

2 shallots, thinly sliced

2 garlic cloves, thinly sliced

1 bouquet garni (see page 159)

Grated zest of ½ lemon

¼ teaspoon piment d'Espelette

1 (750-ml) bottle dry red wine

Fine sea salt and freshly ground black pepper

2 tablespoons extra-virgin olive oil

2 tablespoons / 30 g unsalted butter

1½ tablespoons all-purpose flour

8 ounces / 230 g tomatoes (about 4 large), peeled, halved, seeded, and coarsely chopped

OXTAIL-MACARONI GRATIN

Who doesn't like a good macaroni and cheese on a cold wintry night, when the wind is blowing and our bones are in desperate need of any warmth we can get? I sometimes make mine simple, with just good cheese and a bit of bread crumbs. But from time to time, I prepare something a little more elaborate. Adding oxtail meat to the pasta and topping it all off with a flavorful Comté cheese is not just an improvement; it's a transformation. This is more complicated to make than a simple gratin, true, but it is very rewarding.

IN A DUTCH OVEN or other heavy pot, melt the butter over medium heat. Add the meat and brown well on all sides, about 5 minutes. Add the onion, garlic, thyme, and bay leaf and season with salt and pepper. Pour in the wine and bring to a simmer, then reduce the heat to low and cook until the beef is tender, about 3 hours.

Remove the meat from the bones and roughly chop if necessary. Return the meat to the pot and cook over low heat until the sauce is glossy and thick, about 15 minutes. Remove from the heat and let the oxtails cool slightly.

Meanwhile, bring a large pot of salted water to a boil. Add the macaroni and cook until al dente. Drain in a colander, rinse under cold water, and drain again.

Preheat the oven 400°F/200°C.

Prepare the béchamel sauce. In a medium saucepan, melt butter over medium-low heat. Add the flour, whisking until smooth, then gradually add the milk, still whisking away. Add the nutmeg and season with salt and pepper. Cook, stirring, until the sauce thickens, 8 to 10 minutes. Add the cheese and crème fraîche and stir until the cheese has melted.

SERVES 4

2 tablespoons/30 g unsalted butter, plus more for the baking dish

2 pounds/900 g oxtails, cut into pieces

1 large onion, finely chopped

4 garlic cloves, minced

2 sprigs of fresh thyme

1 bay leaf

Fine sea salt and freshly ground black pepper

1 (750-ml) bottle red wine, preferably Beaujolais

2 cups/280 g small elbow macaroni

For the béchamel
sauce

4 tablespoons / 60 g
  unsalted butter

¼ cup / 30 g all-
  purpose flour

1¼ cups / 300 ml whole
  milk

½ teaspoon grated
  nutmeg

Fine sea salt and
  freshly ground black
  pepper

⅔ cup / 60 g grated
  Gruyère cheese

⅔ cup / 150 ml crème
  fraîche

Grease a 11.5 × 8.5-inch / 30 × 22-cm baking dish with butter. Add a layer of half of the beef and sauce, then half of the macaroni, and half of the bécha-mel sauce. Repeat the layering with the remaining ingredients. Sprinkle with the cheese.

Bake until the gratin is golden on top and bubbling, 20 minutes. Serve immediately.

BLANQUETTE DE VEAU

If I were asked what the quintessential French dish is, I would be tempted to say *blanquette de veau*. I've been having it for as long as I can remember. It's often incredibly aromatic and subtly delicious, but even somewhat bland versions somehow always seem heartwarming. It's one of the foods I find most soothing and comforting. I can't think of a more typical example of bourgeois cooking—meat and vegetables slowly uniting in a tasty winter stew, served over boiled potatoes or rice. It's the sort of old-fashioned dish I think deserves another look.

BRING A LARGE POT of salted water, enough to generously cover the meat, to a boil. Add the veal, return to a boil, and cook for 1 minute. Skim any scum from the surface.

Meanwhile, slice 1½ of the shallots. Stick the cloves into the remaining ½ shallot. Add the carrots, leeks, celery, onion, garlic, all the shallots, and the bouquet garni to the pot, Then add the wine, bring to a low boil, and cook for 2 minutes. Season with 1 tablespoon salt, cover, and simmer over low heat until the veal is tender, about 1 hour and 15 minutes.

Strain the meat and vegetables from the broth and set aside. Discard the bouquet garni. Reserve the broth in the pot.

Melt the 4 tablespoons/60 g of butter in a small saucepan over medium heat. Add the flour, and whisking constantly, and cook, stirring until the roux thickens, about 2 minutes. Season with salt and pepper. Pour the roux into the pot with the broth, whisking constantly, and simmer over low heat until the broth starts to thicken slightly, about 5 minutes.

(recipe continues)

SERVES 6

2½ pounds/1 kg boneless veal shoulder, cut into 2-inch/5-cm cubes

2 small shallots

4 cloves

2 carrots, peeled and cut into chunks

2 leeks, white part only, sliced

1 celery stalk, sliced

1 small onion, sliced

2 garlic cloves, sliced

1 bouquet garni (see page 159)

¼ cup/60 ml white dry wine, optional

Fine sea salt

6 tablespoons/90 g unsalted butter

⅓ cup/40 g all-purpose flour

Freshly ground black pepper

8 ounces/250 g white mushrooms, sliced

5 ounces/150 g pearl onions, peeled

Juice of 1 lemon

⅔ cup/160 ml crème fraîche

2 large egg yolks

A handful of chopped fresh parsley

Return the meat and vegetables to the pot, cover, and simmer for
15 minutes.

Meanwhile, heat the remaining 2 tablespoons/30 g of butter in a medium
sauté pan over medium heat. Cook the mushrooms and pearl onions until
golden, about 6 minutes. Drizzle in half of the lemon juice and simmer for
30 seconds. Add to the big pot.

In a small bowl, mix together the crème fraîche and the remaining lemon
juice, then whisk in the egg yolks. Add a ladle or two of the cooking liquid,
whisk well, and pour the mixture into the big pot. (Do not boil, or the egg
and cream will curdle).

Remove from the heat and serve immediately, garnished with the parsley.

ROAST POTATOES
with HERBS *and* GARLIC

This is the most common side dish in our house. It's on our table practically every day, yet it is always asked for, appreciated, and eaten up. No matter how much of it we have, we always seem to want more. Collectively, the whole family is like a man who's been married to his wife for forty years, had dinner with her every night and breakfast every morning, and is still madly in love with her. There must be something special about her, *non?*

PREHEAT THE OVEN to 350°F/180°C.

Halve the potatoes lengthwise. Put the potatoes, flesh side up, and the garlic on a rimmed baking sheet. Pour the duck fat over the potatoes, sprinkle with salt and pepper, and scatter the sprigs of thyme and rosemary on top.

Bake the potatoes, turning them occasionally, until cooked through, golden, and crisp, 45 to 55 minutes. Serve hot.

SERVES 4 TO 6

2 pounds / 1 kg new
  potatoes, scrubbed

5 garlic cloves,
  unpeeled

4 ounces / 110 g duck
  fat or ¾ cup plus
  2 tablespoons /
  100 ml olive oil

Fine sea salt and
  freshly ground black
  pepper

A few sprigs of fresh
  thyme

A small sprig of
  fresh rosemary

WINTER FEAST

I cherish the calm days of early
January, when Christmas decorations
have found their way back into the
attic and the house feels crisp and
clean and cold. I love to set a table,
adorned with flowers, and serve
old-fashioned, carefully made dishes.
It's a time for traditions.

PEAR FLOGNARDE

This traditional rustic cake, originating in the Limousin region of France, is like a big pancake filled with melt-in-your-mouth pears. It's light and golden and very similar to a flan, which I think of as a custardy cake. I have a particular liking for old-fashioned cakes like this one. In the old Occitan language, *flognarde* means "soft," and it can also refer to a duvet, so you can just imagine how a bite of this feels in your mouth—as light as a feather.

PREHEAT THE OVEN to 350°F/180°C. Grease a 9-inch/22-cm round cake pan with butter.

Peel the pears, cut into quarters, and remove the cores. In a large sauté pan, heat 2 tablespoons/30 g of the butter. Add the pears, sprinkle with 1½ tablespoon/25 g of the granulated sugar, and cook, turning them once, until golden, about 8 minutes. Pour in the rum and simmer to reduce for 2 to 3 minutes. Set aside to cool.

In a large bowl, combine the eggs, the remaining sugar, the honey, vanilla seeds, and salt and whisk until frothy. Melt the remaining 2 tablespoons/30 g butter and whisk into the batter, along with the flour and milk, whisking until smooth.

Scrape the pears and all of their juices into the prepared pan. Pour the batter on top and sprinkle with the brown sugar. Bake until puffed and golden, 35 to 40 minutes. Let cool for at least 15 minutes on a wire rack before unmolding. The cake will deflate gradually as it cools.

Serve warm or at room temperature.

SERVES 6

4 tablespoons/60 g unsalted butter, plus more for the cake pan

6 medium pears, such as Bartlett

⅔ cup/130 g granulated sugar

1½ tablespoon dark rum

4 large eggs

1 tablespoon honey

1 vanilla bean, split lengthwise, seeds scraped out and reserved

¼ teaspoon fine sea salt

1 cup/120 g all-purpose flour, sifted

1⅔ cups/400 ml whole milk

1 tablespoon brown sugar

SARAH BERNHARDT CAKES

Funnily enough, this is a recipe I got from my Icelandic mother-in-law, based on a well-known Danish recipe inspired by a great French actress. As long as we've been going to Iceland for Christmas, we've been having these throughout the month of December, and now I can't imagine the holiday without them. I make them once a year, but they bring back so many fond memories and really put me in the spirit of the season. When I make these chewy, nutty cakes, I always make a lot because they go fast when offered. I keep them in tin boxes in my freezer and take them out about five minutes before serving. That way they are fresh and cold, just the way Santa Claus likes them.

There are no real rules here—you can make the meringues any size you want; I like mine the size of macarons.

PREHEAT THE OVEN to 350°F/180°C. Line 2 baking sheets with parchment paper.

Make the meringue. Whip the egg whites in a large bowl with an electric mixer on high speed until frothy. Gradually add the sugar, 1 to 2 tablespoons at a time, and continue whipping until the egg whites form stiff peaks, about 10 minutes. Gently fold in the almond flour. Using two spoons or a pastry bag fitted with a large plain tip, spoon or pipe the egg whites onto the parchment-lined baking sheets. The meringues should be 1½ to 2 inches/4 to 5 cm wide and ⅓ to ½ inch/1 to 1.5 cm high.

Bake until crisp, 10 to 12 minutes. Let cool on the baking sheets for 8 to 10 minutes, then transfer to a wire rack to cool completely.

(recipe continues)

MAKES 40 TO 50 INDIVIDUAL CAKES (DEPENDING ON SIZE)

For the meringues

4 large egg whites

2⅓ cups/280 g confectioners' sugar, sifted

2 cups/200 g almond flour

For the frosting

2½ cups/250 g confectioners' sugar, sifted

10 tablespoons/ 1¼ sticks/300 g unsalted butter, at room temperature

3 large egg yolks

3 tablespoons instant coffee powder, dissolved in 1½ tablespoons hot water and cooled

1 tablespoon unsweetened cocoa powder

11 ounces/300 g dark chocolate, chopped

Transfer the cooled meringues to a plate, cover with plastic wrap, and freeze while you make the frosting.

Make the frosting. With a wooden spoon, in a medium bowl, mix the sugar with the butter until smooth. Whisk the egg yolks in another medium bowl until pale and thick, then gradually stir into the butter mixture. Pour in the dissolved coffee, add the cocoa powder, and mix until the frosting is smooth and thick. Cover with plastic wrap and refrigerate to firm up a bit, 20 to 30 minutes.

Remove the meringues from the freezer. Use a spoon or a palette knife to spread about 1½ teaspoons frosting over the bottom of each meringue. Return to the freezer frosting side up for 15 minutes to harden.

Put the chocolate in a heatproof bowl. Bring an inch or two of water to a simmer in a saucepan, put the bowl on top, and melt the chocolate, stirring occasionally, about 3 minutes. (You can use the microwave if you prefer.) Remove from the heat. The chocolate should be just warm to the touch; if it is warmer, let it cool a bit.

Dip the frosted side of each meringue in the melted chocolate so the frosting is entirely covered. Let set on a large piece of parchment paper.

Line a large container with parchment paper and arrange the meringues in it, layering them between sheets of parchment. Cover with paper and close the lid tightly. The meringues will keep in the freezer for up to a month.

NOTE: *This recipe uses raw egg yolks in the frosting. We are lucky to have very good farm eggs available to us and I feel confident in their quality. If you do not, use pasteurized eggs, or choose a different recipe when cooking for the very young or old or anyone who is pregnant.*

KOUIGN AMANN

I've spent so many weekends, especially during the cold, rainy months of November and December, taking long brisk walks in St. Malo, where my best childhood friend, Isabelle, has a family home. The sea, the strong winds, the whipping rain, the seaweed smell—it's all most invigorating. And in Brittany, there is so much goodness to look forward to when you come home from one of these walks. The region is renowned for its buttery confections, and I always hesitate between sweet pancakes with a glass of cider or the delicious kouign amann, made from layers of a simple dough folded with butter and sugar. Served slightly warm with, why not, a drizzle of Salted-Butter Crème Caramel (page 278), this cake is a dream come true.

IN A SMALL BOWL, dissolve the yeast in 3 tablespoons of the lukewarm water and let stand until frothy, about 5 minutes.

In a large bowl, mix the flour and fleur de sel and make a well. Add the yeast mixture to the center, then gradually add the remaining 5 tablespoons warm water and start kneading on a floured surface. I do everything by hand, and it usually takes me about 15 minutes of good kneading until I get a soft, supple dough. Shape into a ball and let rise in the bowl, covered with a tea towel, until doubled in size, about 3 hours.

On a floured surface, roll the dough into a square a scant ½ inch/1 cm thick. Spread 3 tablespoons/50 g of the butter on top and sprinkle with ⅓ cup/65 g of the sugar. Fold the corners of the dough into the center to form another square.

(recipe continues)—

SERVES 6

1 tablespoon/12 g active dry yeast

½ cup/120 ml lukewarm water

2 cups/240 g all-purpose flour, plus more for dusting

A good pinch of fleur de sel

12 tablespoons/ 1½ sticks/200 g salted butter, at room temperature, plus more for the pan

1 cup/200 g plus 1 tablespoon granulated sugar

Roll the dough out again until it is a scant ½ inch/1 cm thick, keeping the square shape. You may need to dust it with flour from time to time to keep it from sticking. Repeat the buttering, sugaring, and folding one more time. Wrap in plastic wrap and refrigerate for 30 minutes.

Preheat the oven to 450°F/210°C. Butter a 9-inch/22-cm round cake pan.

Turn the dough seam-side down on a floured surface and roll once more until a scant ½ inch/1 cm thick, keeping the square shape. Spread 5 table-spoons/75 g of the butter on top and sprinkle with ⅓ cup/65 g sugar. Fold the corners of the dough into the center again.

Put the dough into the cake pan and gently press on it with the palm of your hand so it fills the pan. Spread the remaining 1 tablespoon/30 g of butter on top of the dough and sprinkle with the remaining 1 tablespoon of sugar.

Bake until the top of the cake is well caramelized, 22 to 25 minutes. Start checking the cake every 2 to 3 minutes toward the end, as it is so easy to overcaramelize or even burn it. (As I have been making this cake for years, I have learned from my mistakes!)

Remove from the oven and let rest on a rack for 15 minutes before inverting the cake onto a plate. You may need to use a butter knife to help free the cake from the mold. Serve warm or at room temperature.

NOTE: *Should you want to prepare this cake in advance and still serve it warm, I recommend reheating it in a water bath. Return the cake to its pan, set the pan in a larger baking dish, and add 1 inch/2.5 cm hot water to the baking dish. Reheat in a 300°F/150°C oven until warm, about 10 minutes.*

SALTED-BUTTER
CRÈME CARAMEL

I always fool the kids and my guests with this dessert. They think I have made a classic crème caramel, just like my grandmother's. The first time I made it, everyone wanted to know if they were eating panna cotta, a custard, or a cream. It's simply a vanilla custard covered with salted-butter caramel. It always makes everyone very happy.

MAKE THE CUSTARDS. Add 2 tablespoons water to the powdered gelatin and set aside to soften. Or, if using gelatin sheets, soak them in a bowl of cold water until softened; then drain well.

In a medium saucepan, bring the cream and vanilla seeds to a boil over medium heat. Add the sugar and stir until dissolved. Take off the heat and add the egg yolks one by one, whisking constantly.

Pour the custard into four 6-ounce/180-ml ramekins. Let cool completely, then refrigerate until set, 4 to 5 hours, or overnight.

Make the caramel. Melt the sugar in a medium saucepan over medium heat; do not add water, and do not stir until it has nearly completely melted. Then, swirling the pan occasionally, cook until the sugar is uniformly dark amber in color. Remove from the heat, carefully add the butter, stir quickly with a wooden spoon, and return to the heat for a few seconds, then take off the heat again. Add the warm cream, stir quickly, and return to the heat for about 10 seconds, stirring until smooth. Stir in the fleur de sel. Set aside to cool.

Serve the custards topped with the caramel sauce.

SERVES 4

For the custards

1 tablespoon powdered gelatin or 3 gelatin sheets

1½ cups/350 ml heavy cream

1 vanilla bean, split lengthwise, seeds scraped out and reserved

¼ cup/50 g granulated sugar

3 large egg yolks

For the caramel

¾ cup/150 g granulated sugar

3½ tablespoons salted butter

¼ cup/60 ml heavy cream, slightly warmed

¼ teaspoon fleur de sel

MONT BLANC

I've been enjoying this dessert my whole life, usually in cafés or restaurants in Paris. For me as a young girl, nothing felt more grown-up or proper than going to Angelina's and ordering a hot chocolate and a Mont Blanc. It combines so many things that I like—a sense of history and tradition, a bit of flair and chicness, and, of course, chestnut cream. I don't make this classic dessert very often, but when I have visitors from overseas and want to make them feel extra welcome, I will surprise them with a homemade Mont Blanc, just to say *Bienvenue en France.*

6 large egg whites, at room temperature

Pinch of fine sea salt

1 tablespoon cornstarch

1½ cups plus 2 tablespoons / 320 g granulated sugar

1½ cups / 350 ml heavy cream

5 ounces / ⅔ cup / 150 g sweetened chestnut cream

5 ounces / ⅔ cup / 150 g unsweetened chestnut purée

6 candied chestnuts (marrons glacés), cut into small chunks

Confectioners' sugar for dusting

PREHEAT THE OVEN to 275°F/140°C. Line a baking sheet with parchment paper.

Whisk the egg whites and salt in a large bowl with an electric mixer, on high speed, until frothy. Add the cornstarch, then gradually add the sugar, 1 to 2 tablespoons at a time, and continue whipping until the egg whites form stiff peaks, about 10 minutes.

With the help of two large spoons, spoon the egg whites into 6 mounds on the parchment-lined baking sheet. Twirl a spoon in each mound to create a nest-like meringue.

Bake the meringues until crisp, about 1 hour. Let cool completely on a wire rack.

About 20 minutes before serving, whip the cream until stiff. Scoop a few tablespoons into each nest.

In a small bowl, stir the chestnut cream and chestnut purée together. Spoon the mixture into a piping bag fitted with a small plain tip and pipe the

mixture on top of the whipped cream in each meringue, using a spiral motion, as if you were making a nest. Transfer the meringues to the refrigerator to chill for 15 minutes.

Scatter the chopped candied chestnuts on top of the meringues, dust generously with confectioners' sugar, and serve.

CHESTNUT ICE CREAM

When I was a child, one of my fondest memories was the *goûter* hour or afternoon treat. My friends and I were always starving when the school bell rang, and one of the little luxuries we would have was a small tube of vanilla chestnut cream to spread on *pain au lait*, a white bread made with milk. So sweet, so earthy, it satisfied our every need. I always keep chestnut cream on hand at home and somehow manage to squeeze it into just about any dessert I love—chocolate chestnut cake, Mont Blanc (page 280), even pancakes. Sometimes I simply enjoy a large spoonful in the middle of the day. You can buy chestnut cream in some supermarkets and in gourmet shops. This ice cream is my idea of bliss, especially at Christmas time, when chestnuts are traditional.

IN A MEDIUM SAUCEPAN, heat the cream and milk over medium-low heat. Add the vanilla bean and seeds and bring to a low boil.

Meanwhile, in a small bowl, whisk the egg yolks with the sugar until smooth and light in color.

Take the saucepan off the heat and, whisking constantly, pour one-third of the hot liquid over the egg mixture. Then pour the yolk mixture into the saucepan, return to the heat, and cook, whisking briskly, until the custard thickens slightly, 5 to 8 minutes; do not boil. Pour into a large bowl, discard the vanilla bean, and let cool.

Mix the chestnut cream into the custard, then cover with plastic wrap and refrigerate until cold, at least 1 to 2 hours, or overnight.

Freeze the chestnut cream in an ice cream machine according to the manufacturer's instructions. Scoop the ice cream into a container, cover, and freeze for at least 3 hours before serving.

SERVES 6 TO 8

1 cup / 250 ml heavy cream

1 cup / 250 ml whole milk

½ vanilla bean, split lengthwise, seeds scraped out, seeds and bean reserved

3 large egg yolks

¼ cup / 50 g granulated sugar

12 ounces / about 1⅓ cups / 320 g sweetened vanilla chestnut cream

MADELEINES *with* PISTACHIO POTS DE CRÈME

Marcel Proust famously took one bite of a madeleine and was instantly transported to days spent with his aunt in the French countryside. These days, none of us can so much as think of a madeleine without thinking of Proust. But these little cakes have had a special place in my heart forever because they are just so good. I love to serve them to guests, usually after dessert with coffee, as a chic way to end the meal. Sometimes I served them as dessert, but I've found that, delightful as they may be, they don't quite work on their own. So I started pairing them with little custards and have settled on this favorite combination, a luscious pistachio pudding that goes ever so well with both madeleines and coffee. The madeleines are best served straight from the oven.

MAKE THE POTS DE CRÈME. Have ready six 6-ounce/180-ml ramekins.

In a medium saucepan, whisk together the milk, cream, sugar, and pistachio paste and bring to a low boil. Put the cornstarch in a small bowl, ladle some of the milk mixture into the cornstarch, and stir until smooth. Return the mixture to the saucepan and stir until the cream thickens, coating the back of your spoon.

Off the heat, add the egg yolks one by one, whisking constantly. Return to medium-low heat and cook, whisking, until the cream thickens slightly, about 3 minutes. Pour into the ramekins and let cool completely, refrigerate for 5 to 6 hours.

Make the madeleines. Whisk together the sugar, honey, salt, and eggs in a medium bowl until pale and thick. Sift together the flour and baking

SERVES 6

For the pots de crème

1¾ cups/400 ml whole milk

⅓ cup plus 1 tablespoon/100 ml heavy cream

⅓ cup plus 1 tablespoon/75 g granulated sugar

2 teaspoons pistachio paste (see Note)

3 tablespoons cornstarch

2 large egg yolks

For the madeleines

⅔ cup/130 g granulated sugar

2 tablespoons honey

¼ teaspoon fine sea salt

3 large eggs

1¼ cups/150 g all-purpose flour, plus more for the molds

1 teaspoon baking powder

8 tablespoons/1 stick/125 g unsalted butter, melted at room temperature, plus more for the molds

2 tablespoons orange flower water

1 teaspoon grated lemon zest

powder, then gradually fold into the egg mixture. Gently stir in the butter, orange flower water, and lemon zest. Cover and refrigerate for at least 2 hours, or, even better, overnight. It is very important for the batter to be cold—that's what makes a good rounded madeleine with a nice bump.

Preheat the oven 350°F/180°C. Butter and flour two 12-mold madeleine pans.

Divide the cold batter among the molds. Bake until the madeleines are risen and golden around the edges, about 12 minutes. Remove from the oven and use a butter knife to delicately coax each cake out of the mold.

Serve the pots de crème with the warm madeleines.

NOTE: *Pistachio paste can be found in specialty baking stores and online.*

OLD-FASHIONED WAFFLES

I cook most of our family's meals—my dear husband says I've pushed him out of the kitchen! But Oddur makes foolproof soft-boiled eggs and Mia, my eldest, is a little wizard with pancakes and waffles—French, Icelandic, and even American ones. So, on weekends, often the family lets me stay in bed and brings me breakfast. Those are some of my favorite moments. Catching up with magazines, reading books, or pretending to read and actually doing nothing.

My favorite of Mia's waffles is this yeasted French version that we perfected together. They are heavenly with just a sprinkling of powdered sugar, a strong cup of tea, and some peace and quiet. They work really well as dessert as well, with whipped cream or chocolate or caramel sauce.

1½ cups / 375 ml whole milk

2 teaspoons crumbled fresh yeast

2 tablespoons granulated sugar

2 cups / 240 g all-purpose flour, sifted

3 large eggs, separated

7 tablespoons / 100 g unsalted butter, melted

2 tablespoons dark rum

Pinch of fine sea salt

Confectioners' sugar for dusting

WARM 2 TABLESPOONS of the milk until lukewarm and mix with the yeast and sugar in a small bowl. Let sit until frothy, 5 minutes.

Put the flour in a large bowl and make a well in the center. Add the yeast mixture to the well, mix it into the flour, and then gradually whisk in the rest of the milk, the egg yolks, melted butter, rum, and salt until you have a smooth batter.

Whisk the egg whites with an electric mixer until stiff, then fold into the batter, using a rubber spatula. Cover and let stand at room temperature for 30 minutes.

Cook the waffles according to your waffle maker's instructions. Dust with confectioners' sugar before serving.

DAIKON RADISH CAKE

HAPPY VALLEY
WONTON SOUP

RED CHILE SAUCE

BRAISED
SHANGHAINESE
HONG SHAO PORK

TEA EGGS

CHINESE NEW YEAR

It has been a long time since I lived in Hong Kong, but I always celebrate Chinese New Year with my family, no matter where we are. It's part of who I am. It usually falls near the beginning of the year, so it's also a perfect excuse to brighten up our days, do something different, and educate the children. They are French children who go to French schools, but we are all mixed; we have many different cultures and traditions in our blood and I want to keep them alive in our family. I want my children to have some of the same food experiences I had as a child, and I want to cook all my favorite dishes for them. It warms my heart when one of my kids leaves the table with a beaming smile after having eaten some of the same things I did at his or her age.

The food I would always look most forward to having at Chinese New Year was *lo bak gao* (daikon radish cake), a traditional must-have dish thought to bring luck and prosperity, perhaps because *gao* means "height," or "high achievements." Custom aside, I just love the semi-bitterness of the radishes mixed with the delicate flavors of shrimp and mushrooms.

When I was a little girl, my parents had a ritual of hosting a Shanghainese meal on Saturday nights, gatherings with old family friends at a great restaurant, and the food from this province has always been among my favorites. The meat is often soaked in wine, slow-cooked, and then caramelized, and has sweet and sour flavors. A ham hock cooked this way is delicious; the meat literally melts in your mouth, and star anise and cinnamon add such depth. It's a typical family dish, served with freshly steamed white rice. I would always ask the waiter to bring me a plate of beautiful tea eggs to have on the side.

We lived in a neighborhood called Happy Valley in Hong Kong, and it had a restaurant that served some of the best wontons in town. If my parents couldn't find me, they would always start by looking there. I found comfort going there at any time of the day, sharing my table with strangers, and devouring hot dumplings dipped in chile sauce. Just writing about it makes me hungry.

Mango pudding is the one dessert I always made sure to order at a dim sum restaurant. I would quickly look down to the bottom of my order sheet to check the mango pudding box first, then go back up my list, and select the best of the dim sum menu.

With these simple dishes, I give my family a taste of what my life was like growing up.

HAPPY VALLEY WONTON SOUP

MIX THE SHRIMP with the ground pork in a large bowl. Add the egg white, soy sauce, oyster sauce, wine, sesame oil, ginger, sugar, ½ teaspoon of the salt, and ½ teaspoon of the pepper and mix well. Set the filling aside for 20 minutes.

Put a large sheet of parchment paper on your work surface and sprinkle with rice flour. Lay one wonton wrapper on the parchment (keep the remaining wrappers covered with a damp towel as you work so they do not dry out) and scoop a teaspoon of the filling onto the center of the wrapper. Brush the edges of the wrapper with water, fold it in half to make a triangle, and press down firmly on the edges to seal. Gather the 2 opposite corners of the wrapper, dot them with water, and join them together. Press to seal. Set on a flour-dusted baking sheet. Repeat with the remaining wrappers and filling.

Bring the chicken stock to a boil in a large saucepan over medium heat. Season with the remaining ½ teaspoon each of the salt and pepper.

Meanwhile, bring a large pot of water to a boil over high heat. Cook the wontons, in batches, in the boiling water until they rise to the top, 5 to 8 minutes. Transfer to a platter as they are cooked.

Add the wontons to the chicken stock, and bring back to a gentle boil. Ladle about 6 wontons into each bowl and top with some chicken stock. Scatter the chives, cilantro, and scallions on top. Sprinkle each bowl with a few drops of sesame oil and serve the chile sauce on the side.

(recipe continues)

SERVES 10

Generous 1 pound /
  450 g peeled shrimp,
  coarsely chopped

1 pound / 450 g ground
  pork

1 tablespoon egg white

1½ tablespoons soy
  sauce

1 tablespoon oyster
  sauce

1 tablespoon Shaoxing
  wine or dry sherry

1 teaspoon Asian
  sesame oil, plus
  more for serving

2 tablespoons grated
  fresh ginger

½ teaspoon granulated
  sugar

1 teaspoon fine sea salt

1 teaspoon freshly
  ground white pepper

Rice flour or corn-
  starch for dusting

60 square wonton
  wrappers

4 quarts / 4 liters
  chicken stock

10 chives, chopped

3 tablespoons chopped
  fresh cilantro

3 tablespoons thinly
  sliced scallions

Red Chile Sauce
  (recipe follows)

RED CHILE SAUCE

MINCE THE CHILES in a food processor, 1 to 2 minutes.

Heat the oil in a saucepan over medium heat. Add the chiles and cook for 2 minutes. Add the shallots, garlic, and ginger and cook until the mixture is glossy, 2 more minutes. Reduce the heat to low and add the vinegar, salt, and sugar. Mix well, cover, and simmer for 15 minutes. Set aside to cool.

Store the sauce in an airtight glass container in the refrigerator for up to 2 weeks.

MAKES ABOUT
1 CUP/330 G

4 ounces/115 g fresh red chiles, stemmed

1½ tablespoons vegetable oil

6 tablespoons/60 g minced shallots

6 tablespoons/60 g minced garlic

3 tablespoons grated fresh ginger

2 teaspoons rice vinegar

1 teaspoon fine sea salt

½ teaspoon granulated sugar

TEA EGGS

PUT THE EGGS into a pot, cover with cold water, and bring to a gentle boil over medium heat. Boil gently for 12 minutes. Drain the eggs and cool them in cold water, then drain and gently tap the eggs all over with the back of a spoon; be careful not to tap too hard. This will allow the tea mixture to create the marbled effect on the eggs as well as to flavor them.

Pour the water into a large saucepan and add the tea leaves, soy sauce, star anise, cinnamon, orange peel, if using, brown sugar, and the cracked eggs. Bring to a boil, turn the heat to low, and simmer for 3 hours.

Remove from the heat and let the eggs cool at least slightly in the tea mixture before serving. You can let the eggs soak in the mixture overnight in the refrigerator to get more intensity of flavor if you wish; simmer them in the tea mixture for a few minutes to heat them through before serving.

MAKES 12 EGGS

12 large eggs

4 cups / 940 ml water

2 tablespoons black tea leaves

½ cup / 120 ml soy sauce

2 star anise

1 cinnamon stick

2 pieces dried orange peel (optional)

1 tablespoon brown sugar

BRAISED SHANGHAINESE
HONG SHAO PORK

SERVES 4 TO 6

BRING A MEDIUM POT of salted water to a boil. Add the pork, return to a boil, and blanch for 2 minutes. Drain the pork and pat dry with paper towels.

In a wok or large skillet, melt the sugar with the water over medium heat. When the sugar starts to turn slightly golden and caramelize, add the pork and stir to coat it. Remove from the heat.

In a large pot, heat the oil over medium heat. Add the ginger, garlic, and shallot and cook, stirring, for 1 minute. Add the fennel seeds, star anise, cinnamon, cloves, and orange peel and stir until fragrant, about 3 minutes. Add the sesame oil and stir for 30 seconds. Add the dark and light soy sauces and Worcestershire sauce and stir for 1 minute. Add the wine, bring to a simmer, and simmer for 1 minute to reduce.

Add the pork to the pot, along with all its juices, pour in enough water to cover the pork, and bring to a boil. Cover, reduce the heat to low, and simmer until the meat is so tender it falls apart, about 3 hours.

Remove the pork, spices, and aromatics from the pot with a skimmer and set aside. Turn the heat under the pot to high for about a minute or two to reduce the sauce until it is thick and glossy.

Return the pork and spices to the pot, top with the cilantro, and serve directly from the pot or on a platter.

2 tablespoons fine sea salt

3½ pounds / 1.5 kg pork shanks

¼ cup / 50 g granulated sugar

1 tablespoon water

2 tablespoons vegetable oil

10 slices fresh ginger

2 garlic cloves, sliced

1 shallot, sliced

1 teaspoon fennel seeds

5 star anise

2 cinnamon sticks

6 cloves

A strip of orange peel

1 tablespoon Asian sesame oil

3 tablespoons light soy sauce

2 tablespoons dark soy sauce

1 tablespoon Worcestershire sauce

1 cup / 250 ml Shaoxing wine or dry sherry

A handful of chopped fresh cilantro

Steamed white rice for serving

ACKNOWLEDGMENTS

THANK YOU TO:

Oddur, for your beautiful photographs, strong hand, and good advice, and for making me move to the countryside . . . and thanks to all the dogs that made you want to move.

Gunnhildur, þórir, Tiger-Mia, Hudson, Louise, and Gaïa, for eating everything and liking most of it, for bearing with me when dinner was late and when tempers were flaring. And thanks for putting up with your father's demanding photography and for being so helpful with each other.

Johanna and þórir, your encouragement means everything to me.

My aunt Francine; without you, I might never have started to cook.

My fellow Médocains: the generous Fabien and Florence Courrian; Pierre and Marie-Noëlle Aubert, whose kindness is as organic as their vegetables; Monsieur Manenti—how could I cook without your excellent meat?; Francis and Françoise Pion, our snail farmer friends who have saved the day more than once; and Sheyenne, David, Naturel, and Balkis, our constant models.

Jane Butler, for your keen wit and impeccable taste.

Berta Treitl, my agent, for believing in me.

Jenny Beal Davis, for being instrumental in the making of this book.

Everyone at Clarkson Potter, you have been an absolute dream team, especially Rica Allannic, my editor—I am so glad we are on the same page.

And my parents, who, it must be said, made me love food with a deep passion.

INDEX